BIG NARSTIE

HOW TO BE NARSTIE

FOREWORD BY **ED SHEERAN**

EBURY PRESS

1 3 5 7 9 10 8 6 4 2

Ebury Press, an imprint of Ebury Publishing
20 Vauxhall Bridge Road
London SW1V 2SA

Ebury Press is part of the Penguin Random House group of companies
whose addresses can be found at global.penguinrandomhouse.com

Penguin
Random House
UK

Copyright © Big Narstie Limited 2020

Tyrone Lindo has asserted his right to be identified as the
author of this Work in accordance with the Copyright,
Designs and Patents Act 1988

First published by Ebury Press in 2020
This paperback edition published in 2021

www.penguin.co.uk

A CIP catalogue record for this book is
available from the British Library

ISBN 9781529106305

Printed and bound in Italy by Grafica Veneta S.p.A.

The authorised representative in the EEA is Penguin Random House Ireland,
Morrison Chambers, 32 Nassau Street, Dublin D02 YH68.

MIX
Paper from
responsible sources
FSC® C018179

Thank you to all my friends, family and team for your support,
and a big shout out to all the BDL members.
Mai Mai & Tip Drip, Daddy loves you x

CONTENTS

FOREWORD BY
ED SHEERAN

I became a fan of Narstie from Myspace when I was in my teens. I bought his *Drugs and Chicken* mixtape and then his *What's the Story? Chicken Glory*. I became a big fan instantly. I listened to him all throughout my last years of Year 10 and 11 at school, before moving to London in 2008.

Shortly after moving to London, I met Jamal Edwards from SBTV. We struck up a friendship and filmed many videos and he introduced me to a lot of the grime scene that I had been a fan of at school. I remember the first time I met Narstie; it was in Soho House and he complained about all the stairs. I had just come off a tour and had a bit of time off and randomly just said, 'Hey, you wanna stay at mine for the week?' and just as randomly, he said yes.

We formed our friendship that week, in a house I had just bought, with no furniture, only mattresses on the floor. Drinking, smoking and telling jokes with my mates and him. It was really fun.

Narstie has become a very close friend of mine over the years, his family are amazing, his friends are lovely too, and he makes me feel welcome wherever I go.

Over the last nine years of knowing him he's never minced his words, and is brutally honest with me in his opinions; no beating around the bush, just straight to the point. It has been a great help for me at different parts of my career.

This book is your chance to benefit from the same advice that I have been able to count on over the years.

Turn a few pages more and get to read some pure unfiltered life advice courtesy of the King of Base. Hope you enjoy it!

INTRODUCTION

In Brixton, where I grew up, kids would walk out their front doors in the morning and waiting for them there'd be some geezer. When you saw that geezer you'd know: 'That's who I'll be robbing for today.' He'd send the mandem to the West End of London; he'd send them round the local houses. But I'd learned by that point that in life you have to know what you're willing to take, and what you're not willing to take. Man could never send me out there to go and rob on his behalf. From early on, I knew for a fact that I didn't want to be under anyone's wing. I would always be my own man.

I've been thinking a lot about my life while I've been working on this book, and I've realised two things. First: circumstances forced me to become an adult at a very young age. Second: now I'm in my thirties, my life's so good that I feel like I'm having my teenage years right now. I'm like the black Benjamin Button!

Thing is, though, whichever direction you're going through in life, there are points when you have to decide what sort of man or woman you're gonna be, plus how you're gonna cope with life's pains and its joys, and its bits in between.

So who do you look to? Well, when I was seven years old and mad into wrestling, Ultimate Warrior was my fucking idol. I wanted to put paint across my face, put string on my arms and *pump*, just like Ultimate Warrior. I wish I could have been on the receiving end of some of his wisdom. It was not to be, but if you've enjoyed my music, TV or film work over the years then maybe some of what I've learned will make sense to you and your life. (I totally admit that you might not be able to say you've exactly 'enjoyed' my film work if you happened to see me starring alongside Jodie Marsh, Richard Blackwood and Liz from Atomic Kitten in 2016's *Gangsters, Gamblers and Geezers*, which one critic said might be the worst film ever made. And, to be fair, the film was shit. But you've picked up the book now so you might as well just stick with it.)

A few years back I started uploading videos to YouTube where I took the role of Uncle Pain. I only started it as a laugh but my twist on standard agony aunt stuff quickly became the world's most honest advice column, and when viewers started sending in their real-life dilemmas I started to realise just how much everyone was finding life hard to navigate.

The thing with Uncle Pain is that I'm Uncle Pain every day. Me and my mum both have this crazy gift that means when there's people with problems, they just come to us for a chat. Not just friends, either. I don't know why it is, but I'll be in the street or in the shop and it'll be: 'Have you got a light, mate?' Of course. 'By the way, my missus left me and I've lost my house.' Err, okay bruv. 'Also, I've been having an affair!' There's something about me that makes people want to confess their sins. I mean, sometimes I wish they didn't, because it can get a bit awkward when you've just gone in for a Ribena and a donut, but one thing I'll always pride myself on is that I'm honest and true in any situation.

One thing you've got to know about advice: there are two types. Real talk, sometimes the people who give the most advice to others are the last people you should be listening to. They just love the sound of their own voice. No matter what the problem is, they'll just say: 'Believe in yourself, you can do anything.' They'll go away happy and you'll get the warm glow of feeling you've helped someone.

And then … well, then there's the kind of advice that's just the fucking truth. That's the sort of advice you might get from this book, and I'll warn you sometimes the truth ain't pretty. Sure, I could tell someone something to make them feel better about the moment, and they'd be pleased I told them what I did, but if I gave them a rose-tinted perspective they'd be back again in a couple of months with the same problem. If necessary, I will tell someone they're shit and that they need to do something else. What's better? People encourage you to do something you're shit at, so you spend your life hitting your head against the wall? Or someone giving you a kick up the arse and pointing you in the right direction from the get-go?

Now you might say everyone just needs a bit of motivation, but I say you're wrong. Some people do need motivation, but *everyone needs the truth.* If we ever meet I hope you'll be truthful with me, just like I'd be truthful to you, and for that reason you'll find that there's a lot of truth in this book. There's a lot of *life* in this book. If I tried to pretend to you that I'd always been an A1 citizen, all prim and proper, this book would end after chapter two. It wouldn't be worth the paper it's written on. After all, how can I tell you about life, if I'm not being honest?

And yeah, there might be some things we disagree on, but that's just what life's about. I don't like Marmite; I don't eat fish. The fish economy and the Marmite company will never see my money. Are either of them out of business? No. That's because everyone's different. But despite our differences I reckon everyone has a right to experience love, and happiness, and *life.*

This is a book about life. And if you live a decent life that's true to yourself – even if it's not true to the rest of the world – you'll be fine. After all, what else is there? In the immortal words of my mate Andy: you can only piss with the cock you've got.

BIG NARSTIE

Spring 2020

1

SCHOOL:
IF I SURVIVED IT,
YOU CAN TOO

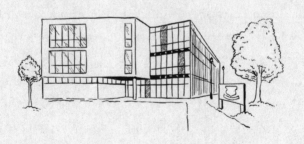

There's a difference between telling someone something and actually educating them. In my opinion, real education can only work if someone's got the means to learn, and by that I mean they need to actually be able to take the education in. If you're thinking about how to keep a roof over your head every night, or about whether you're going to sleep rough next week, it doesn't matter if you go to private school or the local comprehensive because in those seven hours you're just thinking about money.

And what does that do to a kid? Well, for one thing it means your mind isn't on what you're being taught. It's on how you're terrified each night when you go to bed that the bailiffs are going to evict you. It's about how the electricity and gas have been cut off. You're thinking about money; you're thinking about your mum. Even as adults there are times when we look at all the bills on the table and just think: 'Fuck'. And we're adults. Imagine how kids feel.

There's too many kids like that, and I was one of them.

While there's no one-size-fits-all approach to surviving school, I just about got through it in one piece. But, believe it or not, I totally despised school. I remember on those mornings when I'd been refusing to get out of bed, which was most of them, my mum would say to me at the kitchen table: 'When you're older, you'll wish you could go back to school.' And this obviously sounded like total nonsense to young Tyrone Lindo, but, as with most things in life, my mum turned out to be spot on. Older Tyrone doesn't relish the idea of learning about isosceles triangles all over again but he does now realise that school, even with all its crazy bullshit, was a simpler time in life.

Not that it seemed simple at the time. Man, it was hard work, so if you're going through bad times in education now, I know how you're feeling. I couldn't really function properly at school, and not even because academia itself was the hold-back. What put the pressure on was my living situation back home, and the darkness that surrounded it all. The stresses of life were a constant distraction, and I wasn't happy. In fact, a lot of the time I wasn't just unhappy – I was angry. I was pissed, just fucking pissed.

Now you have to remember that when I was at primary school, most of my bredrin's mornings just involved a shower, a bowl of Coco Pops and a walk to school, but my own mornings were a little more complicated because I was going to school straight from what we used to call the madhouse. I'd be up early then I'd accompany my mum to where she worked – a hospital for schizophrenics. I'd find myself sitting in a little fucking room by myself until it was time to go to school. After school, I'd go straight back to the madhouse until my mum's shift was over. My day was bookended by pretty intense scenes.

Harsh but true rule of life: all kids are scumbags, and that's just a fact, but there's different types of scumbags. There's straight-out dosser scumbags, then there's rich scumbags, and the question is this: which type of scumbag are you going to try to align your kids with? Will you align them with scumbags who come from the job centre lifestyle, the underclass world with no economic structural values? Or do you reckon your kids will be better off with the scumbags who have financial backing so that, even if they do fuck up, which they will, their rich grandad will sort it all out? That's the bottom line. And that's how a certain type of scumbag ends up being prime minister, while the other kind of scumbag who went to a normal ghetto school will end up being poor and working in Tesco.

My dad was keen for me to be the posher type of scumbag, but after he and my mum split up my schooling moved to Brixton. The first stop was Santley Primary School, which had started off as a temporary iron structure late in the 1800s and ended up being rebuilt as a massive red-brick monster a few years later. I hadn't been there long before they decided to shut it down (not my fault), and it's now been turned into apartments, which seems to be what they're doing with most big buildings in London.

Slight detour here but can I just say this: the estate agents are trying to sell my old school as being in Clapham, which is insanity because whatever postcode it's got I can tell you one thing – when I was at Santley it was not Clapham, it felt like fucking *Brixton*. Either way, you'll be looking at £650,000 for a two-bedroom flat. Total madness, but not as mad as the fact that anyone would want to make their dinner in the same room I used to shit in. Is it just me who thinks this about massive apartment conversions? Whether it's an old school or an old hospital or whatever, someone's always going to end up living in a former toilet, and it's not as if the estate agent is going to show you round, going: 'Rah, this is the old shitter, that'll be a six hundred grand, please, bruv.' (So if you're ever buying or renting a place, it's worth asking whoever's trying to shift it a simple question: 'Has anyone done a shit in my kitchen?')

But I digress.

After Santley it was off to Glenbrook Primary on Clarence Avenue and then somehow, for my first secondary school, I ended up in St Joseph's, an all-boys Catholic secondary school in Norwood. You might wonder what I was doing in a Catholic school in the first place – I'm a Rasta – but at that time the Catholic schools had the best education, and somehow my dad was back in charge of my education and wangled it, so that's where I ended up.

I didn't cope well in that sort of atmosphere. There was just too much testosterone flying around – and whether you're a guy or a woman you'll probably know exactly what I mean by that. In fact, I lasted just three days, which is how long it took man to get into his first fight. Some older kids from a couple of years above me decided to shove me down a big staircase. I dropped my new pencil case and out fell a pair of those blunt, rounded yellow-handled scissors you have at school. Long story short, those older kids found out that I wasn't the sort of kid they could push around. Short story slightly longer, I got chucked out of the school, and my mum whooped my arse.

Next thing I knew I was at Stockwell Park School. I remember my first day there was gassed – at lunchtime it was Africa vs Jamaica in the football, and there were no school fields or even the fancy Astroturf loads of schools have now. We're talking straight concrete, grazed kneecaps, schoolbags as goalposts: the actual good stuff. But it wasn't exactly St Joseph's. I'll put it this way: I was told Stockwell Park was the first secondary school in this country with metal detectors at the gate, and it wasn't because they were worried about the kids nicking Bunsen burners.

Stockwell Park was a tough school, with tough pupils. I wouldn't say the kids I was at school with were a bad influence on me, but only because my entire *environment* was a bad influence. Imagine what Brixton was like in the nineties, before all the middle-class people started moving into old schools. Back then we were living through the crack renaissance. When I think of my bredrin' back then – Rowdy Bowdy, Sar, Liam, Wes – I'm still in touch with some of them, but most are in prison on crazy sentences: 25 years, 33 years, 42 years. *Big* fucking bird. The rest are dead.

One thing I do have good memories of is the school's epic uniform, which unlike most school uniforms was actually something you wanted to wear. We had black jeans, black Reebok Workouts, a white polo shirt and to top it all off our school's regulation black bomber jacket with a red lion badge. You'd see all these other kids on their way to school in their blazers and hats, and we'd just be hanging out, this group of kids in their black bomber jackets. We looked the absolute bollocks. If you're a parent arguing the toss over secondary schools for your kid, always go for the one with the best uniform. They'll thank you later.

Even so, I'd hear about the posh secondary schools not so far away in south London, like Dulwich College, and when I saw pictures of it I wanted to go there so bad. Let me tell you, there's some proper Harry Potter shit happening in that place. But until I looked into it, I hadn't realised how much the cards were stacked against me: I thought there was a sense of merit, and that if you worked hard you could get into places like Dulwich College. Except places like that are made to keep people like me out. It's, like, £40,000 a year, for a start, so of course, as soon as I found out how much it cost, I realised: fuck that. I was never going there, or anywhere like it. I saw in the paper recently that Dulwich

College sometimes has police outside the school gates these days, and obviously I'm no stranger to seeing cops outside a school but at somewhere like Dulwich College it feels like they're not there to break up fights from the pupils. They're all about protecting the rich kids from the sort of kids who go to Stockwell Park.

And before long I totally was the sort of kid who went to Stockwell Park. When I think back to my schooldays, the first thing I think of is drugs. I was selling weed from my early teens – it's like I was 13 going on 36. It was mad. At the same time, my crew was extorting other kids, making £30 a week just by asking for their lunch money.

At the time it felt like we were just flexing, just doing our thing. We thought: 'At least man can go buy egg fried rice with sweet and sour sauce now, instead of eating shitty school lunches.' I look back on that now, as an older man, and I now think: 'Fucking hell.' I mean, it was bullying, plain and simple. Man was living real barbarian times back then, but it felt like those were the only resources I had around me. I felt like I didn't have any other resources to change my situation, and I felt like I had to be a savage. I don't know if my experience on the stairs at St Joseph's had changed my mindset when it came to standing up for myself, and I know I took it too far, but I just felt like this: was asking nicely going to get me nice stuff? How about sitting in the corner, patiently, hoping that out of the kindness of their heart someone was going to say: 'Ooh, shall I do something nice for Tyrone?' Was any of that going to fucking happen? No, mate.

There was a phrase I'd heard a lot on the block when I was growing up: 'A quiet mouth doesn't eat.' It's the same ethos in the road. Look at all those people in life who have great ideas, but they're little pipsqueaks. The guy who's half as intelligent as them, but has a bigger voice and more confidence, ends up getting the better job. So that's how it felt at school. We were living in the era of Kull the Conqueror. If I could offer my younger self a piece of advice now, it'd be this: don't feel like you have to man up before you even really understand what being a man even is.

At the same time – and this was the big difference between Stockwell Park and my three days with a load of other boys at St Joseph's – there were bare chicks knocking around the place. Most of my friends just wanted to play football but by the time I was 13 I thought I was a big man, and truth be told I was a dirty boy at school. I was trying to use my penis from *early*. What can I say? I just wanted to get it in. Show me a teenage boy who says any different. And then show me his search history.

There were detentions at school, but I didn't care about things like that. Remember, at secondary school I wasn't like a normal 13-year-old – and I wasn't hanging out with my mum before and after school any more. In the four hours after I walked out the school gates I'd be selling drugs to men four times my age. If they tried to bump me I'd threaten to smash them in the head with a brick. When you've been dealing with crackheads with lice and scabies, and you've been in houses with six people who'd rather smoke your weed than bathe their skin, and you've gone home after that, had a bath and pretended to your mum that everything's normal … well, when it came to teachers, they couldn't really tell man much.

While being told off by a teacher in a nice shirt didn't faze me, I only used to really get pissed when they'd write home with letters to my mum. Much as I didn't give a shit about the teachers at school, one person I did care about was my mum, partly because I knew that if she had to come in to sort out some nonsense I'd got myself involved with she'd look at me like she was going to crack my head in right in front of them. She didn't care about what they thought – if she'd been made to come from work all the way down here to the school, just because I'd been a prick, she wouldn't give two shits. She was *regulating*.

Something I did always love with my mum was that it was never a total dictatorship. As a kid, she respected that you had an *opinion*. You could say to my mum: 'Mum, I really don't like how you dealt with that – I think it was mad messed up.' And she'd always give you the reason why you'd made a mistake, then she'd explain why she dealt with you how she did. And she might not have said sorry, but perhaps she might just so happen to cook your favourite food the day after. She treated me like a human being, not just a brainless idiot with no thoughts or feelings. Even when it can seem as if people are coming down hard on you, you always need to look beyond the here and now and see the big picture.

One of the maddest things that happened at Stockwell Park was when the school was due to have an Ofsted inspection, which, as you probably know, is that time of the year when all the teachers start absolutely shitting it because it's finally time for them to be judged on *their* schoolwork. When one of those inspections was due, the head teacher summoned me and my friends to her office for a meeting.

By this point this group of us had a lot of control over the school and if you think that means we were on the student council, well, no. This was a purely badman thing. Except now the head teacher was calling us in and asking us to help with other children in school, getting them to go to their lessons. Unbelievably, they made us prefects! We all did a good job, but the head teacher saw how much power we had over the school so after the Ofsted inspection was over they made a special room for all these temporary prefects, which meant we weren't allowed to mingle with any of the other children in school. It was a pretty extreme measure: we finished school half an hour early, there were no lunchtime breaks at school with the other kids, and we had to eat our lunch in that room. We just couldn't associate with the other kids.

We'd been useful when it came to the inspection, and the school didn't seem to mind the hold we had over other kids when it suited the school's agenda, but when that was over they basically quarantined us. You always need to know when someone's using you. Taking you for a ride. Taking the piss.

Just after they secluded us in school, they brought in some special guys to try to control us. Their names were Hickey and Gilbert – support teachers who could deal with kids like us. And I have to say, big up those guys, because we got on well with them when the head teacher couldn't really figure out how to deal with us. The support guys knew that what you learn in a book isn't automatically the right thing for every situation; they knew that kids had already been half-taught by their parents, and that for some kids this meant they came in relaxed and wanting to learn, but in other cases it was about coming in each morning from fucked up environments. And listen, I might have been a savage back then, but there were other kids whose lives were even more fucked up. Some kids just can't blank all of that out in order to sit and listen and learn for seven hours a day. Hickey and Gilbert understood that and did their best to help, and I hope there are more Hickeys and Gilberts working with kids at schools now. (And if you find yourself your own Hickey or Gilbert, whether it's at school or later on in life, let them help you.)

At the end of the day, and despite Hickey and Gilbert's best efforts, Stockwell Park got rid of me before they should have done, and when I was 15 they packed me off to Vauxhall College. 'We think,' they said, 'you'd do better in a grown-up environment.' I expect what they really meant was: 'We'll do better when you're someone else's problem.'

Both those statements are probably true. Looking back on whether that was the right thing for them to do, I'm in two minds. From their point of view, they obviously just wanted me out of the school.

I remember one teacher actually telling me: 'If you and your mates make it to your mid-twenties, I'd be astonished.' A teacher actually said that to me! It was like they'd given up on me.

One thing I do know is that when the *South London Press*, my local newspaper, took me back to my school a few years later, that same teacher was so embarrassed I'd done well that they didn't even want to come and meet me. They were totally ashamed, although I do admit that maybe if I hadn't had a few lucky breaks later on they might have been right. Maybe I really was destined, at one point, not to see my mid-twenties. Like I say, most of my mates from back then are now either dead or in prison.

Either way, maybe Stockwell Park dumping me on other educational establishments really was the best thing for me. From my point of view, I found that the colleges and centres I was attending were more interested in catering towards my interests and aptitudes. As well as Vauxhall I was spending time at Brixton College, and community projects like the Bootstraps community centre in Stockwell and the Norwood Centre – these were places for troubled kids to get a handle on academic learning, but where we'd also learn some practical skills. Sometimes life's all about finding the situations that fit in around you, instead of situations where you're the one who has to fit in.

The later part of my education didn't work for everyone, and, in fact, I remember that on one of our courses, of twenty people in the class I was one of only three to graduate. But, for me, it kind of did the trick. There were smaller classes, with tutors who knew how to handle us.

It's funny how much more interested you are in learning when it's something that actually interests you, rather than just sitting there while some mad geography teacher drones on and on about oxbow lakes. I studied engineering, and sound engineering, and even did a little plumbing course. This felt like proper, actual stuff you could use in the real world! I've never had to negotiate an oxbow lake, but I've fixed a couple of leaky radiators in my time. (Bonus tip here – you can fix 80% of household annoyances if your DIY box contains nothing more than screwdrivers, spanners, duct tape, a can of WD-40 and a tube of decorator's caulk.)

Like I said earlier, it seems to me that one of the biggest problems with the education system is that teachers have to treat every kid in their classroom as if they've come from the same mindspace and headspace when they walk in the door. But everyone's come from a different household, with different things on their minds. Example: there are kids who care for their parents, and start each day looking after adult relatives. It's like having a full-time job, then going to work all day, then having another full-time job afterwards. Imagine your mum's had a mad episode and nearly died and things, and then you have to sit in a classroom and try to act all normal. Or you're about to lose your flat. How can that kid have a fighting chance of studying in a normal quiet environment? It's fucked.

If you're lucky enough never to have dealt with shit like that, nothing I say can really describe the stress of trying to keep a roof over your head – especially when you're a kid, and you feel like the responsibility is all on your shoulders. I had a friend at school. His mum was crazy; she couldn't work, or wouldn't work, but the point is she didn't work. From the age of nine years old, my mate had to somehow come up with a tenner a day for the electric. He was nine years old! And he had to come up with ten quid from nowhere. And that's why he would rob, and do all sorts of barbarian shit. It wasn't right, and he didn't want to be doing it, but he wanted to help his mum and his little sister. For him, and for thousands of kids like that who don't choose to be in that situation, it all comes down to the algebra of life: it's fight, or it's flight. And it's not something they choose.

Do the teachers take that sort of madness into account? Well, let's be real: are they even *able* to? There are definitely some shit teachers knocking around but most of them are good people who are just overworked and underpaid, so it's not their fault. Things are even worse now than they were when I was at school. You hear about teachers these days who are taking in fruit and sandwiches for poorer kids, just so those kids will have something decent to eat. But in schools like the ones I grew up with, where every kid's poor, and you've got half the class turning up each morning with rumbling tummies, how can teachers cope? Especially when schools are having to run internet crowdfunding campaigns for basic shit like books and pencils.

So obviously, more money needs to go into schools. And with that, you'd get teachers who were actually able to teach each and every kid in a way that made sense. With some people, you can say: 'Here's the textbook, here's your paper and pens, figure it out.' With others, it's more like: 'Alright, I'll show you with some bullet points on the board, then you can get on with it.' Other kids just won't get it and they don't understand the book at all, and those are the ones who need the most teaching. The sad thing is, they're the ones who never really get the teaching. They just get left behind.

I was never the pupil who could work from a textbook; I just sat there and played with my phone because I didn't understand what was going on. I ended up doing alright for myself. In every class in the country right now there might be a genius who just needs a bit of help. Everyone deserves a chance to show their ability.

So if I'm ever made Education Minister, which is unlikely, particularly given what I say about politicians later on in this book, I'll make some big-arse changes. More cash for schools is the first step, particularly in the current political climate when no fucker from abroad is going to want or be able to bring their knowledge to the UK, and we need to start training up our best brains right now.

A teacher, for many kids, is no different to a substitute parent: you're providing children with skills to take them ahead through their mature stages of life. So, of course, we all agree that if you don't know how to read or write you're fucked, and if you can't do numbers how are you going to know if someone's trying to bump you or not? That sort of knowledge keeps us all safe. Likewise, history's important – this is how we know who we are, and where we are, and why. But are kids taught enough about the things that are happening around us right now; the things that people will learn about in future history lessons? How did Donald Trump become president? Why did Brexit happen? And why is someone who makes racist comments allowed to become prime minister?

But I'd also want to see – for the right kids, and the kids who are being left behind or bored shitless by endless banging on about the assorted wives of Henry VIII – more practical stuff being taught in school. Like how to start a business, or even how to open a bank account. When teachers were spending all their time teaching me about algebra

– something I would never, ever use – why didn't they teach me how to open a bank account? Why aren't kids taught how payday loans are a con?

Also, you need to put food in your fridge, but you also need to know what to do with that food. It might sound stupid, but what about more cooking? Fair enough, people used to think food tech was stupid when I was at school, but I think that's probably the best life skill you can take with you. Do you know how many people can't boil an egg? They can't fucking cook! Being able to cook a Victoria sponge is one thing, and, to be honest, it might have come in helpful for me when I took part in the celebrity version of *Bake Off*, but, for those of us who are never going to be the next Mary Berry, how about just learning the basics on how to cook a decent meal that's cheaper, more healthy and tastier than something from your local chicken place? I mean, there's not many things tastier than decent fried chicken so that's probably a bad example, but you get my point: you're not going to get home after a hard day at work and start drawing perfect equilateral triangles.

Anyway, rather than sit here at my laptop setting the world to rights, I'm looking into actually putting my money where my mouth is, and I'm in the process of trying to set up something like a Windrush open school. It's a lot of stress and a lot of headaches, but I'm working with one of my teenage mentors, Pastor Chris, and his mate, Pastor Alton, on developing the idea – Pastor Alton is already the head teacher of a private secondary school, so he knows how this whole thing works. I want it to be a fully inclusive school funded by a truly diverse range of people, and open to all colours and creeds.

It's a pretty simple idea: why can't a bunch of successful black people open up a school that understands our community and understands our kids?

In my mind it's a standard educational school that's able, if it's appropriate, to steer people into creative spaces. Maybe it'll all come to nothing, but I look at it like this: how can I help as many people as possible? Maybe I'd drop in and bust out some motivational speeches, or help out the music and acting departments. Any encouragement is good, I think, when you're a teenager, and I truly believe the school could change the life of everyone who went to it. That's the sort of legacy I'd like to leave behind.

Sometimes I wonder if I'd do my schooldays differently if I was given another chance. I'd be less of an arsehole, for a start, but, until someone invents a time machine, at least I know that, against all the odds, I've become a regular at one of the country's poshest universities.

A couple of years ago the Oxford Union invited me along to give them a couple of speeches – I was surprised when I was asked to do it, and even more surprised when they asked me to talk about some real G shit. They wanted to hear from me about my life and how I saw life in general. In one of the talks I ended up chatting about Shakespeare and Kanye West, and I was a bit freaked out because what with it being Oxford they've got loads of dead people buried in the floor of the debating chamber, but I styled it out and they've been asking me to go back. That's the sort of encouragement I needed from my teachers back in the day.

Hopefully it's encouraging to you now, though, that this Brixton street kid made it to Oxford University in the end, and he didn't even have to pay Dulwich College £40k a year for the privilege. So much for not making it past 25 …

2

MONEY:
IT'S ALL ABOUT
MINDSTATE

Different people will look at money in different ways. Think about a ten quid note, and the way one person will know that's how much they have to spend on food for the entire week, while another person will blow it all on a sandwich, a coffee and a muffin on a trip to Starbucks.

Now think again about that person in Starbucks. It's okay to have a treat from time to time, but ten quid to them is disposable money and that's not the right way to be looking at it. It's all about mindstate. Fact is, some people will see a pound coin as something to be spent, while others – and I'm now one of these people – will see its potential to become something bigger.

I'll give you an example. When I was 16 and still at college, I qualified for this thing called the Employment and Support Allowance – basically, your ESA was where the Government would give you £30 a week. Bare man used to just spunk their ESAs on chips and fizzy drinks, but I didn't touch mine for months, until it was nearly £800, and I used it to buy my first big bag of weed. Every 16-year-old had the same £30 per week, but I allowed mine to grow into £800 and then I turned that into £2,500.

Or look at it another way: me and you could each get
£50 this week, but that doesn't mean that at the end of the
week we're each going to have the same amount of money.
You could just live off the £50, but I could bank £40 and
live off the remaining tenner – and you'd be surprised how
far I can make ten quid go. There's a mindstate that sep-
arates who's going to be up and who's going to be down,
and it's not about how much money you have. You could
be the queen's kid, and you could have the secret service at
your beck and call, but you might still have no idea how
to use your cash. You could have a billion pounds in the
bank but if you've still got a hundred quid mindstate, you'll
carry on being poor.

On a bigger scale, imagine I could do a show tomorrow
and make a hundred grand, or imagine walking out your
front door, kicking some old bag that's lying in the gutter
and finding a hundred grand in it. However it happens, fact
is we've each got a hundred grand. Think about this: one
month later, will you still have a hundred grand, or will it
now be sixty grand because you've taken a little holiday,
you've given your mum some money and you've got yourself
a new watch? Are you just intending to live off the hundred
grand until it's zero grand? Meanwhile, I've made a couple
of investments here and there, and I've now got twice what
I started with. (What I'd probably do, if you're wondering,
is a bit less risky: I'd put £60,000 in my savings, then try to
turn the remaining £40,000 back to £100,000.)

How you approach money might depend on where you're from – but where you're from doesn't need to define where you're at right now. I recently played golf for the first time – a weird sport, with too much walking involved, and, considering it's supposed to be relaxing, I found that trying to hit that tiny ball just made me really fucking angry. If you're thinking the idea of me on a golf course seems weird, I can assure you it all came about a) by accident and b) in the pursuit of food. Long story short, I was having a lunch meeting, the nearest restaurant was on a golf course, everything got out of hand, and the next thing I knew I was at the wheel of a golf buggy chasing after balls I'd accidentally walloped into a hedge.

I wouldn't have imagined 20 years ago that I'd even be taking a business meeting, or at least not one that made sense at a golf club, and it's true that I was the only black face in the entire place. But here's the thing: this might sound arrogant, but these days everywhere I go I feel like I'm supposed to be there.

Now, I'm a strong believer in the secret of positive energy, as well as the idea that you'll miss your blessing if you don't think you're deserving of a blessing. Sometimes you need to ignore the inner you – the you that's urging you to shy away from blessings. You need to believe you deserve all the blessings that are coming your way. But what about when there's not much in the way of blessings coming your way? When there are no blessings to be found? When you're in the *zero-blessing zone*? If you're poor, should you feel that's somehow deserved, too? No, bruv, you should not. But that's a lesson it took me a while to learn.

I remember I once got angry with my friend Sugartits. You need to know that Sugartits comes from money. BIG money. His parents are super-rich: every year his family would go on three holidays. Disneyland, skiing, the whole shebang. (By the way, you can always find out if someone's posh by asking them if their parents ever took them skiing. Posh kids' parents *always* take them skiing.) So I said to Sugartits once when we were out in some flash bar: 'Bro, sometimes I don't know how much I'm enjoying myself doing certain things.' I was talking about the lifestyle I'd found myself in, where I'd often end up in these fancy places. It was all a far cry from what I'd grown knowing around Acre Lane in Brixton, know what I mean?

And he went: 'Like a lot of people from your way of life—' FROM MY WAY OF LIFE! '—because you're not used to having money, and because you didn't come from money, and because you don't get the whole concept of carefree spending, you can't adapt to these places easily.' He looked me up and down, then said: 'You come to places like this, but all you do is smoke weed.'

His point was pretty plain. I was doing what I'd always been doing, just in flashier places. My circumstances had changed, but I hadn't. Swanky nightclub where a drink and mixer is £28? I'd smoke a spliff. Posh meeting? Smoke a spliff. It was my way of fitting in on my terms. Obviously, I didn't fit in at all and I stood out like a sore thumb. Sugartits, on the other hand, knew how to behave in these situations. He was comfortable being spendy. So while I'd responded to getting a bit of money by feeling I could take my daughter to Hamley's, or taking her swimming, which was just pretty modest and basic stuff I never had, Sugartits was frying bigger fish. He wouldn't think twice about hiring a yacht and doing the Mediterranean. He'd never consider whether he fitted in, because he'd been brought up with those visions and experiences in his head. I'd never had that life, and money can't buy you a sense of belonging.

So yeah, I got angry with Sugartits when he said that to me. Not because he was wrong, but because he was right. What he said was just too truthful.

Chances are, you've felt the same way at some point in your life. If you've ever ended up in a fancy restaurant with a menu you can't understand, have you felt inferior? A rich person would either know straight off the bat what the menu said or they'd have the confidence to go, 'Oi, waiter, what does this mean?' But someone like you or me might just end up ordering the only dish whose name we know how to pronounce. We sit a little bit lower in our chair, don't we, in places like that. We don't want anyone to notice us, in case they realise we're not supposed to be there. Madness.

Or think of a kid whose family has only ever had money for the basics, compared with a kid whose parents took them on holiday every year. I bet the first kid, when they eventually did have enough money for a holiday, just wouldn't be able to relax in the same way. They might actually spend most of their holiday more stressed out than if they'd stayed at home! They'd feel like they simply didn't belong in a holiday situation. Even when they had the money, they'd feel like a fraud.

That's the wrong mindset! The right mindset – and it took me a while to realise this – is that you need to be just like me on that golf course: if you find yourself somewhere, however strange it might seem, that's the place you deserve to be. You're there, so you're supposed to be there.

Anyway, I never want to change as a person just because I've got a few quid now, but Sugartits did have a point: until a few years ago I was still living with my old hangups about money. For a while, even when I was winning, I still felt like I was suffering. It sounds stupid, but it's like post-traumatic stress from being raised poor.

Things hadn't been easy for us growing up in south London. As I said earlier, my mum was a registered nurse who worked in local schizophrenic hospitals, but she also did cleaning jobs out of hours, then, after a spell as a support teacher in a local school, she went back into nursing. She worked hard, and she worked long hours, but there wasn't much spare cash in the house. Sure, there was food on the table – but not for all of us. I remember seeing my mother drink hot water for dinner, so there'd be food for me and my brother. She would go without food, just so I could eat.

There are two big things I learned from my mum when it came to shopping. Firstly, if there's any little bargain on the shelf, you snap it up. Two-for-one on bog roll? Buy as much as you can carry and shove the spare packets in a cupboard: it's not going to expire, and you're not going to stop shitting. Yellow stickers on expensive meat? Fill your basket and chuck it in the freezer for a rainy day. I still do that today, whenever I see a bargain.

Secondly, sometimes there'll come a point when you've worked hard enough, and maybe a few bills have been a bit lower that month than you were expecting, and you can have a splurge. My mum would work nightshifts for two months straight, without a day off, but then one day she'd say: 'Put on your trainers, we're going down the high street.' I remember she said that once when I was about twelve and I thought we were going to get some meat, but we walked straight past the meat place and ended up at Cash Converters. We walked in and she just went: 'Remind me, which computer did you want?' And five minutes later we were walking out with a Super Nintendo console. I guess that's how it's supposed to be done: you work hard for what you want, so that when you eventually get it you feel rewarded and it actually means something.

Of course it's not as if my mum wanted a fucking Nintendo. As I got older I started to think about the fact that she never, ever splurged on herself – just like when she'd have hot water for dinner, she'd go without so that we could sometimes have things *we* wanted. It made me feel guilty, but then I got older still, and I became a parent, and I realised that sort of shit's just the fundamentals of unconditional love.

You need to look at it like this: when you become a parent your own happiness is directly related to your kids' happiness. You don't realise this until you're a bit older – in fact it might sound fucked up and weird – but when your parents buy you something they're living through you. Even though my mum had gone without, she was content to see the happiness on my face. (Now I think about it, my mum was probably also being her usual smart self with that Nintendo console: she knew that if I was in front of our telly, I wouldn't be out on the street causing chaos.)

I now experience that feeling of happiness when I can give things to my own kids. When you buy a skipping rope, it's not for you – it's because of how happy your daughter will be in the garden once you've handed it over. Actually, it's even cheaper than that with my daughter. She goes apeshit for any balloon, so when I'm getting petrol from the local BP I'll grab all their promotional balloons from outside, bundle them in the back of the motor and surprise her when I get home. As far as she's concerned that's the biggest present in the world. Seriously though, who doesn't like a balloon?

My mum's side of the family was poor but well connected – there might not have been a hundred quid in her bank account, but there was always someone coming round with two boxes of Rice Krispies, some rice and a pound of meat. My dad's side of the family, on the other hand, had more money but they were fucked because they simply weren't well connected.

My dad gave me his own lesson in money, but maybe not the sort of lesson he'd intended. After he and my mum split up, he wanted me and my brother to live with him, and put the decision onto us. Which was a dick move anyway, but there you go. When we both chose my mum, figuring we'd rather be poor and with her than wealthy with him, he basically cut us off, but every couple of weeks he'd take us up to Oxford Street on shopping sprees. I think he was expecting that after a while we'd decide we wanted every day to be a shopping spree, and that eventually we'd choose to live with him. But we never did. Each time, it'd get to six o'clock and we'd just take our new trainers and get the Victoria line straight back down to Brixton, back to our mum's place. He didn't understand that.

So that taught me a lot about what money can and can't buy, and it means that with my own kids I know spending quality time with them, and showing they're loved, is more important than flashing around a credit card. There are no shortcuts when it comes to family, and while I learned a lot from how my dad approached money, I wonder if each time me and my brother went home to my mum it was my dad who learned the biggest lesson of all. Money does open a lot of doors and it does impress a lot of people but it can't replace loyalty, and love, and a bond between mother and son.

In a funny way I now realise that it was a privilege to see my mum be hard-working, and that's something I want to pass on to my own kids.

With my money, I'm trying to set it up for my children so that there are conditions in place, meaning that they can't fuck up my money even if they want to. They can't touch it until they're a decent age, for a start, and even then it comes in stages.

Too much money, and no idea about what it means, will absolutely destroy kids. It's true that I want my kids to have more than me, but I also want them to experience hardness, and to understand what money is, and to know that whether you have it or don't, life's never an easy ride.

The right way to look at each pound coin is as a seed that could grow into a money tree. Back in the day, like any kid who kept being told they had no future, I used to play the National Lottery once in a while – but as time went by I found that I had more faith in my own plans than risking a nugget on the Lottery.

And we've all seen what happens when people win the Lottery. (It's also often what happens when celebrities get their first big chunks of cash.) They buy a pub, even though they've never run a pub. They open a restaurant, even though they don't know how restaurants work. They buy a speedboat, a luxury car, a fancy holiday. The businesses fail, the flash possessions are sold to pay off an unexpected tax bill, and then it's bankruptcy and divorce. When people gain big sums of money really quickly with no sense of growth, common sense goes out the window and nine times out of ten they lose it. Time and time again, they lose it all.

How many people do you know who've had money in their lives, but their mind was wrong, so now they're skint? The money itself wasn't the problem – the problem was what they decided to do with the money. Having money is no different to using the internet; whether it's good or bad is all about how you approach it. In the right hands, with a positive person, money can set up a food bank or a women's refuge, but in the wrong hands it'll get spunked up the wall on drugs. In the right hands the internet can inspire millions; in the wrong hands you'll go down the rabbit hole of heinous shit on the dark web.

Do I like money? Yes, I do, especially when it's pink and papery, but I'm never going to lose sight of the fact that after a certain point, once you've got food in your fridge and shoes on your feet, it's just an empty vessel – and what happens after that comes back once again to your mindstate.

The main problem, like I said before, is that we're not taught about money when we're at school – and the older you get, and the further away you get from school, the more you realise how ridiculous it is that we never learned about any of this stuff. The idea that credit cards aren't free money, for instance – how many of us had to run up massive credit card debts before we realised how hard it was to get out of debt, especially when there's 20% interest being added month, after month, after month? We didn't learn how to budget, or about investments or ISAs. The information that the education system gives kids to go out into the world with is pitiful – it's almost like we're destined to fail.

One thing you'll hear a lot about money, usually from people who've got wads of cash piling up at home, is this: 'Money can't buy you happiness.' Now listen, I get what these people are trying to say, but while I agree money won't guarantee a trouble-free life, it can definitely make your life easier. People who say money can't buy happiness are probably people who've never experienced the unhappiness of having no money at all. You've got a roof over your head and food in your fridge? That'll make you happy if your family's been starving. You don't have to work three jobs, which means you get to see your family and friends? Yeah, that'll make you happy, too, if you've had to work through every birthday and special occasion.

I don't say that because I think money cures everything, or even because I think people without any cash must always be unhappy, but because so much financial advice seems to come from people who've never looked poverty in the eye and seen a life of despair staring back at them.

One thing that's also true: Biggie wasn't lying when he said that with mo' money come mo' problems. You'll notice, if you keep your eyes open, that while certain people in your life – the ones it's worth keeping in your life – treat you exactly the same as they always did, others start to look to you as a lifeline as soon as they get a sniff of cash. It's subtle, sometimes. You'll be in the pub and they'll look to you for the next round, even though you bought the last one; at the club, you'll notice that after a night of bottle service, they'll let you settle the bill.

I must confess I've got no patience for friends who are like that around me. I'd happily go to the cashpoint, with-draw some notes and give a homeless man a hundred quid, because that could make a big difference to someone who's living with his sleeping bag in the rain and has nothing. And when I say nothing, I don't just mean no money, I mean no options to even make money. When I see man down on his face without a castle, I feel like I should help him because I'm in a better position, and I often do. But at the same time, and naming no names (Paul), I'd resent giving my mate a score when he's got a roof over his head and the only reason he's skint is that he's got a shit work ethic. I see him – I'm his mate! I see how he lives his life. He's got options; he just can't be bothered to act on them. That's where the irritation is.

So if you do come into money – even if it's just a modest wage, but especially if it's big money – your biggest task is to look at the structure of people you've got around you. Most people with money end up in a situation where they're surrounded by yes men: a load of broke cunts who depend on you for their livelihoods, whose advice and concern is motivated purely by how scared they are about their nest egg. Instead of telling you the truth, they'd rather keep you cool so they can carry on getting paid. And fair enough, everyone's got bills to pay, but that's the music industry in a nutshell, and it's the way real life works too.

It can be alluring to have a yes man agreeing to everything man's doing even though they know it's wrong, but everything will come back on you eventually. That's why one of the rules of the Base Defence League is: thou shall not turn a blind eye to fuckery. Other BDL commandments include: respect the tun tun; death to rapists, nonces and paedophiles; and thou shall not be a cunt. (To be fair, the greatest money advice I could give right now is that you could have saved yourself the price of this book by just printing out the BDL commandments off Google Images, but it's too late now so cheers for the purchase anyway.)

Make no mistake: money makes people do crazy things. I've seen it with my own eyes. So for example, what if I told you right now that you could become a millionaire by tomorrow evening?

It's easy, really. All you need to do is find any weapon you can, nick the nearest car then drive to your local bank. You hold someone with a knife until you get your million quid, and then there's probably some sort of shoot-out with the cops and a few people die, but for a brief moment, standing in the street with a sports bag full of notes, there you are: a millionaire.

There was probably a point in that last paragraph where you started thinking: 'Hold on, you crazy old cunt, what are you talking about?' And some readers might have put the brakes on a little earlier than others – that's fine, I'm not judging – but the point is most of us, by the end of my money-making scheme, would have bailed. With good reason. As my mum used to say: 'Not all money is good money.'

Truth is, everyone has a choice to be a millionaire overnight, but the question is whether it fits in with your moral code, and whether you could live with the consequences. You could pull off that bank job and there's nothing to stop you – except your moral code and the way you choose to live your life as a human being, and whether you'd risk putting your family through the nightmare of you ending up in prison for the rest of your life. Even if you got away with it, could you look your children in the eye when they asked how you paid for your house? Would you be proud of that? The answer is surely no.

So if you're after money to make yourself happy, getting money the wrong way – getting what my mum would call bad money – defeats the whole point. Take it from me: I've been desperate, and I've done things I'm not proud of for money, and it didn't end up making me happy. Would I do any of it again, knowing what I know now? No, mate.

I was lucky, in the end, but I know not everyone gets the same breaks I got. I want to try to do something about that.

Over the last few years I've been getting into Bitcoin and trading. Again, not the sort of thing they teach you about at school, and I didn't know what the fuck I was doing to start with, but I started with small investments and that was probably for the best considering the first few went totally tits up, but within my first month I'd made my first successful trade. I made a grand total of £12.50 profit, but the actual sum didn't matter because it was all about the feeling of having made a successful trade. It felt like I'd made £250,000.

That got me thinking, and (though it's in its early stages) I'm in the process of creating an app, and the idea is that it'd be for anyone – teens, single parents, people who are coming out of prison – to make their own trades and be their own boss. You get a demo account to trade with fake money, so you don't lose on your first investments like I did, then once you've made £1,500 in the demo account I give you £300 of real money. That's when you start trading properly, and away you go.

It might sound ambitious, but I have a vision that one day you'll be walking down the street in Brixton or Peckham or anywhere you'd usually see kids hanging round on their phones, and the kids will still be on their phones but what'll be different is the apps they'll have open. Instead of using their Samsungs or iPhones to check their socials, they'll be buying and selling shares in Samsung, Apple, Facebook and Snapchat; all those companies they're already involved with every day, anyway.

When you make money, even if it's just £12.50 to start off with, you instantly become an entrepreneur, and I want to play a small role in creating a new generation of entrepreneurs, who'll maybe make apps of their own in the future, or teach the next generation how to manage their money. Maybe I'll bump into them over a round of golf.

And so it all comes back to changing our mindsets when it comes to money. Being financially poor is one thing, but being poor in terms of experience, knowledge and self-awareness is what really does us in.

We spend so much time thinking about what we're worth in terms of money in the bank, and lose sight of the fact that what we're really worth comes down to our value as humans.

That's something you can't ever put a price on.

3

FAME: HOW TO SURVIVE IT WITHOUT LOSING YOUR MIND

One of the maddest things about fame, and something that sums up the whole idea of fame, is that the more famous you get, the more free shit comes your way. Just because you've been on the telly, it doesn't automatically mean you've got a pot to piss in back home, but generally speaking most famous people can afford to buy their own shoes. So what happens when they play a show, or take a meeting? Box-fresh sneakers. Fucking piles of them! Bare free clothes, free food, free booze, free everything. Get this: you get to the point in your life where you can suddenly afford to buy stuff, and then you don't need to buy it any more.

The more money you earn, the more you get for free. It's like you're being paid twice. Of *course* famous people look immaculate the whole time – they're not out there sniffing whatever's in their laundry basket each morning, because their clothes are arriving on the back of a fucking motorbike!

It's like the business exec who gets paid £3m plus bonuses and she gets a company car to and from the office every day: free travel. But who's stuck paying for a Travelcard each day so they can get a bus to and from their three minimum wage jobs? People so skint they can't even afford to eat at the end of the day. I mean, I'm not saying I intend to turn up at my next gig on the bus, and for the record I'd very much like to continue opening the door to surprise clothing deliveries, but it amazes me how arse-about-tit the whole fame thing is.

And the reason I mention all this is that I know how alluring the whole thing looks, but it's all fucking fake. If you're 14, or 24, or fucking 84, the best advice I can give you is this: don't get caught up in trying to live the lifestyles of the rich and famous. When they've got a red carpet event coming up, they're not spending their Saturdays in the posh bit of Westfield where the security guards give you dirty looks for merely stepping foot in their shops. Their clothes are gifted; their jewels are borrowed.

When you're a kid you don't really understand what fame is or how it works, but there's a point when you realise what's behind it all and my first lesson in fame was brutal but important.

You know when you were younger and you really idolised someone? With me, as a kid I was mad into wrestling: WWE, WWF, Wrestlemania, the whole lot. Whether it was Hulk Hogan, Jake 'The Snake' Roberts, the Undertaker, I wasn't fussed; if there was some geezer in spandex chucking a table at someone, I was into it.

As an eight-year-old I felt as if I was part of the franchise. I wanted the Undertaker to become the heavyweight champion of WWF and do the Royal Rumble; I saw him fight Jake the Snake. I saw the whole build up and the entire journey. I believed in what they were doing and I wanted to be part of it. And it wasn't just me – all my mates at school were down with wrestling. It gave us all something to believe in.

I probably believed a little too much. It all came to a head, and by that I mean it literally came to my cousin Ramone's head, one afternoon when I was playing wrestling at home and decided to smash Ramone round the face with the end of a chair. As you'd expect, my mum took exception to this and during the ensuing argument, when she was going apeshit at me, I said: 'Why can't man do it when the Undertaker does it?'

My mum's reply hit me with the force of, well, the end of a chair. 'The Undertaker *doesn't* do it,' she said. 'It's not a real chair. The reason your heroes get back up again is that they're faking it. None of it's real.'

So you can imagine the scene: Ramone's out cold on the floor because I've smashed him with a wooden chair, my mum's shouting at me, and little eight-year-old me is feeling totally broken. He's finding out that everything he thought was real was a lie.

Even if you weren't into wrestling, you probably know the feeling, because we've all experienced the sensation of something we thought was real being unmasked as fake – whether it's Father Christmas, the Tooth Fairy or the concept of Boris Johnson wanting what's right for the country. It's a bit like that moment when you're growing up and you realise, without even realising you're realising, that your parents don't know everything and that they're fallible. It hits you for six.

For me, finding out that wrestling was staged was an early lesson in fame, and an early insight into the fact that all fame is a con. I'll be blunt: Beyoncé might be Beyoncé, but she still goes for a shit twice a day.

When people become famous quickly it fucks with their head so I'm lucky that in a way – and I know this might sound cheeky – I've always been famous, although not always for the best reasons. I come from what you might call a popular family. My brother was well known in the local area and some of my older relatives had been prolific criminals, and with that came what I'll call 'criminal popularity'.

On top of all that, add in all my other uncles, aunties and cousins and it was impossible to walk through Brixton without being stopped for a chat for one reason or another, and, as I got into my teens and started doing stuff on the street, I myself became popular locally for some quite different reasons. So when my music took off, and people would recognise me for that, the fame that came with it was something I already knew how to deal with, just on a different scale.

These days I find myself dealing with the more well-known kind of fame, and there's nothing to say that you won't find yourself in the same position. Look at Alex from Glasto: one minute he's with his mates watching Dave perform at a music festival; the next thing he knows he's on stage, live on BBC TV, a trending topic on Twitter and within weeks he's releasing his first single and doing night-club PAs. And if you don't remember Alex from Glasto, that's just an example of how quickly things move these days. In the era of social media we're constantly a hair's breadth away from fame – whether you fire off a tweet that goes viral, or someone turns you into a national hero when they film you standing up to a racist on the bus, fame can come quickly but so can a lot of the shit that comes with it.

The first thing you need to remember, and I've had to remind myself of this a few times over the years, is that having a career, being successful and being famous are three very different things – and that's before you even start thinking about things like personal fulfilment and actually being a decent human being. Like, you could climb on top of a crane, start waving a flag around then do a big shit on the crowds gathering below, and you'd probably get a half page in the next day's *Metro*. (A bit of free advice: do not do that.) Or you could go on next year's *Love Island* and be the world's biggest arsehole for a month and a half, and you'd get a full page. Or if you wanted the front page, you could get caught trying to pull off the next big diamond heist in Hatton Garden. (Don't do that either – that's where my personal jeweller works.)

There are loads of ways you could get your name in the paper, but if fame's something you like the sound of, you should at least have a go at earning it through doing something proper, and doing it well. However famous people might get, the ones who keep their careers going have got some sort of talent at the heart of it all. I never would have got my Channel 4 show if I'd never been fucking funny on TV before, and I never would have been on TV if I hadn't have done online shit like my Uncle Pain advice videos on YouTube, and none of that would ever have happened if I hadn't thrown my heart and soul into grime back in the day. And *none* of that happened overnight.

Money didn't come overnight, either. And for some people you consider famous, it never comes. There are young kids you've never heard of – that I've probably never heard of – and they've got millions of views on YouTube and loads of people know them, but they're still in the hood. They have a million quid's worth of fame, but only a hundred pounds' worth of money. Tom Cruise is fine: he's got the bank balance to support his fame. But how about some new kid on the grime scene whose songs are blowing up, but he's still living in his mum's box room? There are more of these people than we realise: people who are heroes with nothing in the bank.

Being famous doesn't automatically make you rich but I'm not saying it doesn't have its perks. I've probably been guilty of taking it all for granted myself a bit: for me fame came gradually, almost without me realising it was really happening. But when I stop and think about it all, I think celebrities should be more open about the hollow side of fame. That'll stop a young 14-year-old kid stealing because they want to be like man. I've seen mad things – kids trying to keep up with this lifestyle, thieving and robbing to get to this place that's not even real. Trust me. That guy behind the curtain, in the *Wizard of Oz*? With fame it's not a wizard, and it's not even a little man. It's a dog eating its own shit.

But fame is seductive, and it's hard to keep your head on straight when everyone around you falls for its charms.

I played a club show not so long ago and they were rolling the red carpet out for me: 'Whatever you want, sir! Yes, sir, no sir' – the full production. But I could see that the staff who worked there were being treated like shit, and even though I had an infinite bar tab, all the people who were working the event were being charged a fiver a drink. I double-checked with the organisers: 'Do I have an infinite bar?' They said yes. 'Then in that case, my infinite bar is for the people working here.'

The organisers looked well pissed off, but I said to them: 'Don't be super-nice to me for one day, and horrible to the people you work with every single day.' I just didn't want to turn a blind eye to things I knew were wrong, and it ended up making the event more of a success: the team was on fire that night (I mean, they were all off their faces by about halfway through) and now I know that if I ever need anything in that area I've got a few people who might give me a hand. If you're famous and you're turning a blind eye to fuckery, you're helping create monsters.

Obviously, if I'd gone in on any normal night and told the bar managers that they needed to give their staff free drinks all night, they'd have told me to fuck off – and that just underlines my point about not being seduced by having your balls tickled by the fickle hand of fame. When I'm booked for a show, from 24 hours beforehand until about 20 minutes after, the world is my oyster. Anything I want is all cool, and nothing is too much trouble. As soon as that 20 minutes is up, I've done my job and I've been paid and I could literally be on fire and nobody would care. I could be running around the backstage area with flames coming out my arse and the organisers would just be focusing on the next performer.

As long as I continue to remember that, there's no problem – problems come for famous people when people don't understand that. It's like they're surprised that it's people's jobs to be nice to them. With me, it's more like: 'I appreciate your attention – but you've just paid £50,000 for me to come to your show so of course you're going to be nice!'

I suppose there's something here that anyone can find useful: don't be fooled by people when they're on their best behaviour. I had a mate who was out with me at some celeb event: everything's paid for, everything's laid out, there are women everywhere, drink's flowing, perfect scenery, and all eyes were on us.

He was like: 'My missus is boring. Blah blah blah, these girls here are nicer.'

I said to him: 'Don't mess up your home for a fairytale world.' He didn't know what I meant. I was like: 'These girls here who are treating you like a celebrity – they've never seen your dirty boxers in the washing basket in the morning. They've never seen you when you haven't had a shave in two weeks and you're just sitting in your pants playing *Call of Duty*. They're seeing you when you've just had a fresh trim, when your beard is fluorescent and glistening in the light and you've got girls in bikinis bringing sparkling bottles of alcohol to you. That's the person they like. They don't know you.'

But he went with one of the girls anyway. He messed up his home, obviously. And guess what? After three or four weeks of seeing the real him, this new girl didn't like it. My mate wasn't happy with this. He thought his new girl was a gold-digger. I was like: 'No, mate. You're a catfish.' I mean, they were both idiots in that situation – in a way, both he and she had been seduced by something that wasn't real.

Another big reason you need to approach fame with caution, apart from ensuring you don't turn into a massive cunt, is that there's no knowing when fame – and success – will come to an end.

I always find myself quoting that bit from the original Spider-Man films: 'With great power comes great responsibility.' But there's another bit people don't always remember, where the Green Goblin's got Peter Parker trapped on top of some building, and he tells Peter: 'They found you amusing for a while, the people of this city. But one thing they love more than a hero is to see a hero fail.' You'd be surprised how quickly the rug's pulled from under someone's feet, and all the support from fans, the media and everyone else suddenly disappears.

I remember when I was working with Craig David on 'When The Bassline Drops' – I was round his studio and all the gold and platinum discs for his records were in the toilet.

I was like, 'Bruv, why are all these motherfucking plaques in the toilet?'

He said that they were all for his old stuff, rather than for his new stuff. He said they had no weight. Now, you need to remember that back in the day Craig David was one of Britain's most successful musicians, but after a few years he sort of withdrew from the public eye quite a bit. There were parts of the media that underestimated Craig and had him written off as a has-been, and he only really made a big comeback a few years ago. So I guess you could sort of understand why he felt the awards for his older stuff weren't so much part of his story these days. But I'm afraid that when he told me that I lost it.

'Bag of shit!' I went. 'You're a badman, fam, do you know who you are? You're motherfucking Craig David, fam! I was fingering girls in the park drinking watermelon Bacardi Breezers trying to sing your songs, you fucker! Talking shit about these plaques in the toilet? Don't get me mad, fam! You paved the way for guys like me to even want to do music! You went INTERNATIONAL with English-sounding music! No American could have made "Fill Me In"! That's straight out of the United Kingdom! Never feel ashamed! Never downplay your success! You're iconic! You're a pioneer! That's why I'm here! FUCKING TOILET???'

Long story short, he took his awards out of the toilet and hung them back up, but it's no lie that when the media decides to flip on you, it can get horrible. I'm fortunate in a way to be in a position where nothing anyone can write about me will ever faze me. There's no headline that could ever put me through more trauma than I've experienced in real life. Put it like this: I've seen man's head blown off their shoulders, and you're talking about a newspaper column, or an email? Do you think an email's going to make me lose sleep, when I've seen pink brain and dark matter fly out of a man's skull? I've seen my bredrin' die on the fucking stairs – negativity in the media will never faze me, because I come from the hard stuff.

That's not to say I didn't have questions about fame when I first started out. With weed, for instance, I had a feeling before I made the decision to be in the public eye that because everything in life comes with a price, and because I felt like the price of smoking weed would be negative coverage, I should try to pretend I was super squeaky clean. So when I first started doing music, I tried to be reserved and I tried to hold everything back. Thing is, it didn't work because it didn't show who I am. Truth be told, I'm loud, I'm noisy, whatever it is, I say it is; and yeah, I smoke weed. I don't have a filter – I just say what I think, and while it may be right or it may be wrong, at least I know I've been honest. After I decided to be myself, things started happening for me. As soon as I started to show who I really was, my career started to fly.

It's pretty freeing, knowing you don't need to keep up a pretence. With fame, just like in the rest of everyday existence, my philosophy is that anything you hold as a dirty secret will be used against you, and if you don't embrace who you really are, people will find things to hurt you with. As the saying goes: tell the truth, and shame the Devil. I'm known around the world as a big weed smoker but, because I don't treat it as a dirty secret, nobody's got any leverage over me. And that means that when the media take a photo of me outside an awards show smoking a massive biffter, it's pointless for them to write about it because the whole fucking world already knows about it anyway.

Now, for me, being so popular for being myself is the best reward. But I accept that being yourself is not an approach that's going to work for every Tom, Dick and Harry Styles. In general, you'll find that most people who end up being famous achieve their fame, or maintain it, by using some sort of alter-ego, or by presenting just one specific part of their personality. The famous person we see on TV isn't really the same person who gets home and puts the bins out. And for most people I'd say that's a pretty good way to approach fame: if you give the public every little part of your existence, so there's no part of your being that's just for you and your family, you'll start to feel pretty hollow.

And if you keep things separate, it means you're less likely to allow the fame to end up defining who you are. Fame's the same as youthful good looks, money, and (for fellas, anyway) a luscious hairline: if you build your entire being around it, you're fucked if one day it's not there any more.

Fame should be seen as the colour you paint your front door, and the posh lampshade you have in your entrance hall, not the foundations of your entire house – fame might be the first thing people see, but it's not what's keeping the whole thing together. Of course, if you're a fan – whether it's of wrestling, a musician or the latest lad to come out of *Love Island* – it's worth remembering that *what* you see isn't necessarily *who* you see. In the words of Tupac: 'How can you have love for a stranger?'

Still, there are a few people knocking around who've found a way to be straightforward about who they are in the public eye, in a way that doesn't drive them round the bloody bend.

One of those is Ed Sheeran, who I've known for *time*. Since long before he ended up becoming one of the biggest artists on the entire fucking planet. I remember a point a couple of years ago when I was just starting to blow and it looked like my street notoriety and underground success might be paving the way for a different sort of fame, and Ed gave me some really important advice.

He told me: 'Bro, now you're starting to get bigger, and fans will come up and ask to take pictures, there may be a day when you're having a bad time and you're not wanting to take pictures with anyone. But try and suck it up. For that moment. Take the picture.'

I asked him why, because my initial reaction was: 'Fuck that – if I'm pissed, I'm pissed, and they ain't getting no photo.'

And the way he explained it – well, it wasn't really just about taking photos, it was about how we behave as famous people. He told me to really think about the situation. 'Think about this person who has only ever seen you on TV, and how this will be the first and probably last time they'll ever meet you. You might have done selfies with a thousand other people before them, and they could all have come away thinking about what a cool guy you are, but this one person won't know about the thousand other people. They'll know about them, and you, in that moment, and how you made them feel.'

I sat back and analysed it and thought: 'Rah, that's fucking deep.' Nobody else knows you've had a bad day. You need to give them that moment. And – fuck the fame chat for a minute – that's actually advice that makes sense in every aspect of our lives. Whether it's some geezer on the bus, the girl serving you in KFC or the traffic warden giving you a parking ticket, they can only judge you on how you are in that moment you're with them. So be kind, and when it's the first time you meet someone think about how it might be the last time, too, and what sort of image you want to leave them with. Actually, ignore the traffic warden part of that. Fuck traffic wardens. But my point stands.

This also means thinking about what you're doing when you're out and about in public. The most embarrassing place I've been recognised is a sex shop in Soho – which, like a lot of Soho sex shops, seems to be in the basement of a book shop. Do they start with a sex shop and put a book shop on top for respectability? Or does the book shop come first, and they have to chuck a sex shop underneath to stop all the old pervs hanging around the book shop's erotica section?

Fuck knows, but basically my mate Obi (aka Kevin Legend) went into the book shop part to buy a mafia book, and while I was waiting by the door smoking a massive joint some old bloke gives me the nastiest look imaginable, as if I'm the scum of the earth. But where does he go? Down the stairs, into the sex shop. And I thought: who's he calling a scumbag? So I followed him downstairs, as you do, past the £800 vibrators that looked like something out of *Star Trek*, and there were TVs everywhere showing pregnant women having sex and all manner of debauchery, and I found this geezer and made eye contact with him, just to say: 'Don't you judge me, bruv, when you're down here planning your next wank.'

Once I'd made my point, I made my way back up the stairs, and right on cue I made eye contact again – this time with a group of school kids who were passing the shop. 'OH MY GOD!' one of them yelled. 'IT'S BIG NARSTIE!' Not exactly my finest hour.

I don't know if those kids were fans or just people who recognised me (and this is something you need to remember – being famous doesn't mean people actually like you), but I find 'fan' to be quite a weird word, anyway. When I created the BDL, which anyone who liked my work could be part of, it's because I never felt comfortable when people would say 'those are your fans'. For me, there shouldn't be a hierarchy: every BDL member is one of my peers. I had a few lucky breaks and their own lucky breaks might be ahead of them, but I always feel like I could easily be in their shoes; and, who knows, maybe they could just as easily be in mine.

And I'll be honest, treating BDL members as equals has had its perks. The best of the lot has to be the time

I was standing at the till at a petrol station having just chucked £70 of petrol in my car – I was distracted because I was having an argument on the phone at the time and I managed to put the wrong PIN in the machine three times in a row, which meant instant lockout. So I was stuck, miles from home, with no way of paying. The guy behind me in the queue? Turned out to be a BDL member who paid the £70 for me, which makes me think two things: 1) This was a solid guy; 2) He's probably got more money in the bank than I have. Point is, when people treat you with so much love, I think it'd be rude to just call them a fan. I'm lucky that the people who follow my work are people who seem to really care about me. Hopefully I'm repaying that by really *being* me. You don't have to be famous to do the same: if people show you genuine love in life, repay them by being totally *you* with them.

And if people go a bit wobbly or star-struck around me? I'm in no position to judge others for how they behave around famous people – when I met Raleigh Ritchie, the singer but also the guy who played Grey Worm in *Game of Thrones*, I got so carried away calling him Grey Worm in the studio that he looked like he wanted to punch me in the face. Meeting people through my Channel 4 show and all the appearances I make on other programmes has opened me up to meeting loads of random people: Judge Rinder's a deep cat and a fucking badman – intellectual as well as nice. Stephen Fry, also, is a total fucking G, and has the confidence of a person who's totally comfortable with everyone. Ian Wright: absolute legend.

But it was when I first met Sizzla in Jamaica that I found myself getting pretty awestruck. I wasn't shy exactly, but I found myself becoming a LOT more talkative – my voice was going at a thousand words a minute and I kept saying things like: 'Oh my God, you're so fucking sick!'

It was probably how the eight-year-old me would have behaved around Hulk Hogan. In fairness, there was just something about Sizzla's whole aura and demeanour, and I think a lot of well-known people could take a leaf out of Sizzla's book. He feeds roughly 700 families in his community; every time he does a feature on someone else's song, the money he makes goes to feeding the families in that community and building the community's infrastructure. That geezer's bought 15 motorbikes for other people! That sort of use of fame and success is so deep, and so powerful, and so spiritually lifting. THAT is power. So yeah, I was in awe of Sizzla.

I know most of the things you'll hear about fame tell you that it turns you into an arsehole, and in most cases that's true, but as you can see from examples like Ed and Sizzla, it's not a given. When people first come face to face with the fame game they need to decide whether or not they're going to live by a moral code. And you can't invent a moral code – I mean, that's not moral in the first place. For me, the moral code I'd show you is the same moral code

I'd show my mum, the same one I'd show my missus, the same one I'd show Pastor Chris. My actions might change depending on how you behave, and what sort of moral code you're working to, but my bar is set in a certain place. It'll only move if you're the one who moves it.

I guess one thing that comes with fame is the idea that you're going to be seen as a role model, and I have to admit that's something that does my nut in. Example: I was a tear-away from Brixton, but I need to recognise now I've got a media profile; people from the UK and all over the world have started listening to my music and they're liking what I represent. That makes me feel uneasy sometimes because I know that if it looks like I'm saying, 'Oi bruv, fuck education, just smoke weed and sell drugs and you'll make it', then some kids might do that.

So it's up to me to make a responsible decision in my head and say: 'Rah, doing all that isn't the way to do what I've done.' And yeah, it's true that before all this I was just an angry, confused, fucked up black kid from the ghetto. One of millions just like me. Then I had a lucky break, and another one, and another one after that – and luck had to be part of it because, like I say, I'm one of millions. But remember, plenty of kids who did the same things I did ended up dead or in prison.

When it comes to the idea of being a role model, then, whether it's through fame or just being well-known in your local community, the question is: if you're a fucked up person yourself who's just had a lucky break or three, how can you set an example for other people? What should I say? 'Wait and see if you're lucky or not'? I guess some people would misunderstand my success and think: 'Rah, Narstie's message is that you get famous and successful by being a savage when you're young.' And I get why some people might think that, but if you've bought this book (or even nicked it) I reckon you're sharp enough to know what I'm really getting at, which is this: I've done alright for myself *despite* everything I went through, not because of it.

And when I got out, I stayed out.

The smartest people I've known from my days in Brixton have all shown me that the moment when you're out of the situation is not the time to carry on doing it: it's the time to stay out, to be grateful for whatever platform you now have, and to use that platform to make sure other people don't have to do the same things you did, see the things you saw, or lose the things you lost. I've done a lot, seen a lot and lost a lot, and for better or worse some of that did make me the man I am today, but I really believe that none of my success, or my fame, is down to my transgressions as a teenager.

I know I'm incredibly lucky to be famous for the right reasons, and more than *that* the most remarkable thing is that I'm famous for being myself. Throughout it all I've managed to make sure I've kept my friends and my family close.

Whether or not you end up being famous for five minutes, five seconds or not at all, one of your ultimate goals in life has to be that the people who are around you are around you for *you*. And that you have them in your life because they're *them*. As for me? I'm still surrounded by people who won't think twice about calling me a fat shit, and long may that continue.

4

FATHERHOOD: BREAKING THE CYCLE

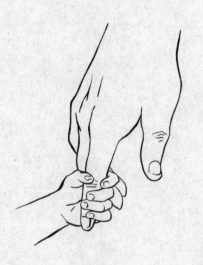

One thing being a parent has taught me is that there's no book on how to be a dad. I mean, don't get me wrong, there are thousands of books on how to bring up kids and plenty of authors who'll happily take your cash, but I've yet to find one that really sums up what's going on for parents, or how your life changes when another life enters the world.

If I was writing a parenting book, Chapter One would advise all parents-to-be to find some time for themselves before the birth, to take a newspaper to the bathroom and to enjoy one long, last, shit in peace, because that'll be your last opportunity for several years to enjoy the majestic serenity of a long leisurely dump without some miniature human crawling, strolling or running in for a chat. Going to the toilet once you've had kids is like trying to have a shit in prison: no privacy whatsoever. Allow me to shit in peace!

I've also learned that while most kids end up eventually becoming their parents, others have to learn how *not* to be them – and the real question at the centre of that is whether or not you even realise you need to break the cycle.

Fatherhood is something that snuck up on me. Up until about five years ago, life was all about me, myself and I. (Well, and my missus.) I didn't understand the emotions of being a parent, or why you'd want all that hassle. In the mornings and afternoons I'd drive past all the parents doing the school run, dragging their screaming kids to and from school in the pissing rain, and I'd think: 'Look at these fucking idiots!'

Now, in 2020, with two kids of my own, I'm one of those fucking idiots, and no word of a lie: I couldn't be happier.

But I'll tell you what, there's nothing like becoming a dad yourself to make you ask some questions about your own father and the relationship you had with him.

When I was a kid, and I'd talk with my mates about their dads, there were a few with happy experiences but mostly they seemed to fall into two camps: the kids who were sad because their dads weren't around, and the kids who were sad because their dads *were* around – but were arseholes. Looking back, I drew two short straws on that front. My dad was around until I was about six – my big brother, being a few years older than me, remembers those early years in the house as being pretty happy. But after 18 years of marriage, he and my mum went through a break-up, and during that time he was an arsehole. Then after that, when he wasn't around, I only had on-off contact with him, and he was an arsehole then too. Double the arsehole, double the pain.

My dad was all about appearance. When I was younger I wasn't allowed to wear tracksuits when I was going out to play with my friends – these items were strictly for when I was doing PE at school! At the heart of this fundamental misunderstanding of the concept of streetwear, my dad's opinion was that even if I was kicking around the house or going down the corner shop for a pint of milk, I had to look smart at all times. It says a lot about my dad's priorities that when I was in my teens this was one of the few areas where he'd still put money into the household I shared with my mum and brother: paying the electric bill might still have been a headache for us, but there I was in a Ben Sherman shirt and Paul Smith shoes. All my mates had tracksuits, and I was the only person out robbing in loafers and shirts.

His brothers and sisters – my aunties and uncles – are all Yardies, but my dad saw himself as proper English, and he went to great efforts to concoct what he thought was an appropriate demeanour. He had a strict regime: manners, politeness, the rights and wrongs of how to do business.

He did well in business, too. What I was young it seemed like my dad was doing intergalactic stuff: he was running clubs in the West End, and for a while he was the personal bodyguard for Jeremy Joseph, the guy who ran G-A-Y, the country's biggest gay club. When I'd go out with my dad to clubs, and he was off working, my babysitter was a seven-foot French trans woman called Galaxy, with piercings all over her face and the alien from, well, *Alien* tattooed on the back of her head. She'd grab me drinks, crisps and anything I wanted, as long as I didn't stray out of the back office.

One thing I'll always remember is me and my dad driving back from my Uncle Beef's house in my dad's old Ford – Beef used to breed Rottweilers, and my dad used to breed pit bulls, so they'd been having some sort of dog-related discussion. Halfway home there was a minor road rage incident with another motorist, and the other guy got out of his car, giving it all that. I watched from the passenger seat as my dad got out of our car, walked in front of the bonnet and basically thumped this other guy's Adam's apple straight out of his neck. Man started foaming from his mouth and dropped to the ground, and my dad simply grabbed him and rolled his body to the side of the street. Then my dad got back in the car and we drove off.

He said to me: 'Boy, are you alright?'

I just burst into tears.

And then my dad, he got mad with me: 'Boy, what are you crying for? Did *you* do something wrong? Don't you fucking cry!'

Now, looking back from the vantage point of adulthood there's a lot to unpack in all that. Stuff like: what did he think he was doing smashing up some man's throat in front of his little kid? Did he think he was setting me a good example, showing me how to deal with a problem? Was this him showing how a 'man' sorts things out?

But it's his response to me crying that really makes me wonder what was going on. He was a big believer in the 'men don't cry' bullshit so maybe he just wanted me to man up or some bollocks, but at the same time, I wonder now if there was a moment when he got back in the car and saw me crying, when he suddenly in a split second realised what he'd done. Not just what he'd done to that poor fucker on the side of the road, but what he'd done to me.

One thing you need to know about bringing up kids is that you can't really pick and choose what they'll remember when they're older, or what stuff will end up being part of their personality. Example: you can spend hundreds of quid on making their fourth birthday totally memorable, hiring in clowns and balloon artists and throwing money at lavish gifts, but there's every chance your kid won't remember it, and their only memory of being four might be something totally random, like the time they were walking round Asda and a box of Cheerios fell off a shelf onto a man's head. Or maybe they will remember the party! Truth is, everything probably means something. I wouldn't say my dad was exactly an expert in the complexities of child psychology but fucking hell bruv, seeing your dad smash up some bloke over nothing? That's the sort of thing a kid never forgets.

Maybe he didn't care. At times he seemed to be making a point of raising me to be a very militant and soldier-like person, even when he was also trying to instil crazy morals in me. I guess for him there wasn't much of a jump between 'being polite', and 'you always talk to a person while looking directly in the eye', and 'never lie', and more extreme stuff like 'never whimper away from an argument'.

But it came unstuck when he was telling me about the stuff of what a 'real man' is supposed to do. In theory, a lot of what he was saying was spot on: you never leave your family behind, you always do what needs doing to defend your family, and so on. They were strong values. The only problem with him banging on about those values, and going out of his way to instil them in his kids, is that he himself went the opposite way.

For a start, he'd left me, my mum and my brother behind when they split up – fair enough, there's always going to be one parent who has to move out when a marriage breaks down, but the way he'd wanted me and my brother to choose between him and my mum, putting that decision on us, was out of order. Maybe when he was telling me all this stuff he was trying to make sure I didn't make mistakes he'd made himself, but to me it just seemed like he was being a hypocrite. It's as true for parents as it is for any sort of relationship – you need to be consistent.

Later on, when I was 13, I was round my dad's place and I had an altercation with him over something stupid. Boom: it fucked me up. And in turn it fucked up our already fucked up relationship forever. I'll always remember the last thing he said to me that day: 'I don't want to see you until you're twenty-one.'

World's most obvious parenting tip: don't say that sort of shit to your kids. But I mean, I was still a kid back then, so I was like: 'I don't give a fuck. I don't want to see you either.'

And that was that. My Uncle Ninja picked me up and took me back to my mum's, and from that age I never saw my dad for years and years. But I did see him before I was 21. Two years before his deadline, when I was 19, one day quite out of the blue my mum said to me: 'Your dad's dying. He's got cancer.'

To begin with I just didn't care – I didn't want to see him, and I knew he didn't want to see me. To her credit, considering this was years after she and my dad had split up, my mum explained to me that things with my dad had changed, or more specifically that *he* had changed. She said he wanted to make an effort to put things right. Hearing this, I felt like in an instant my anger and resentment was starting to fall away. I remember thinking: 'Cool. He wants to see me. So I want to see him.'

So that's what I did, and off I went on a late night visit to St Thomas' Hospital. Remember, from 13 to 19, I'd been without him. As you get older you start to feel like six years can go in the blink of an eye, but in your teens that six-year period is totally pivotal in your transition from being a kid to being a man. It's when you become the person you're going to be for the rest of your life. My dad hadn't been around for that important period; I'd done it myself. I was alright now. I didn't need him.

But when he called me on my way to the hospital, asking me to pick up some proper yard food on the way because the hospital food was total shit, it was the first sign that this next stage of our relationship wouldn't be about how much I needed him. It was about how much he needed me.

Nothing summed that up better than the fact that after I arrived at the intensive care unit, and I saw him lying there in that hospital bed, and for the first time in my life I felt sorry for my dad, I ended up having to take him to the toilet and wipe his arse for him. I don't know if you've ever been in a similar situation – and I do know that plenty of kids work as carers for their parents, so it's not as unusual as it might seem – but let me tell you this, nothing shines a light on the relationship between father and son quite like wiping your own dad's bumhole.

The significance of the moment, and the reversal of roles in that hospital toilet cubicle, wasn't exactly lost on my dad. He broke down in tears and started to apologise – for the situation we were in right there and then, for the situations he'd put me in since I was a kid; for everything.

In the weeks that followed, his health improved and in time so did our relationship. We started getting things back on track, and I'd check in on him more and more frequently, helping him out with bits around his house. I became his part-time carer, until he didn't need a carer any more and could focus on repairing our relationship.

He showed me some good stuff in the period that followed. He was running some strip clubs at that point, and used to do protection work for loads of the Chinese clubs in Soho. He took me to one of them for my 20th birthday, an evening that ended abruptly when I got nicked smoking weed in his car outside the venue. There I was getting nicely high in the car; next thing I know there's a policeman knocking on the window and it's off to Regent Street Police Station. My dad's response was pretty funny, all told: 'I suppose you might as well make your own way home.' Cheers!

But it wasn't long before the cracks in our relationships started to show again. The first sign things were going tits up was when he and his sister had a massive argument over some bullshit or other, the upshot being that he told me never to talk to my auntie again. If I saw her on the street, I had to ignore her. He was telling my whole family that they should walk past her, and not even talk to her kids.

I was like: 'Dad, you know we can't do that.' He didn't understand, so I explained: 'You've raised us never to be disrespectful to our family, or disrespectful to our elders. There's no time in my life when you'd have accepted me standing there slagging off my auntie, or walking past her. You wouldn't tolerate that, so we're not going to start doing it now, are we?'

Well, you can imagine, this line of argument went down like a cold bucket of sick and we had a massive barney.

Then things took an extreme and unexpected turn for the worse. I'd just moved to my first place in Essex – an old flat bashed together by a crap landlord who hadn't sorted out the damp. There was mould everywhere, and I'm not going to turn this into a science lesson but the long and short of it is that when you're sleeping around mould, spores get in your lungs and fuck you up. That flat nearly killed me: one of my lungs collapsed and left me with a swollen heart. It came to a head when I blacked out, and when I woke up I was in a hospital bed, having been in a coma.

By this point my other half had obviously been phoning round my entire family and, without knowing about my dad's falling out with his sister, she'd phoned my auntie. Get this: when I came out of my coma, the first thing I had to put up with was my dad having a go at me about my missus phoning my auntie. I couldn't believe that was all he cared about. He was more preoccupied with that than the fact that I'd almost died. It's like: mate, I know families are complicated, but there are times when you put disagreements to one side, and I'd say your son almost dying is one of those times.

Anyway, from that point, shit with my dad went back to how it had been for most of my teens. It spiralled back into fuckery and the relationship I had with him never recovered. I remember feeling pretty stupid for letting him back in my life, and regretting not listening to my gut instinct when he'd first wanted to get back in touch.

From that point on, we were as distant as we'd been during my teens.

And then one day in the spring of 2017, he died.

This'll sound strange if you've had a close relationship with your own dad, but when mine died I didn't feel much. I guess I'd already lost him plenty of times in my life: when he moved out when I was six, when we fell out when I was 13, when we fell out again later on. I'd had plenty of practice when it came to the idea of him not being around. And plenty of practice when it came to not caring. I'd always advise people to do everything they can to repair relationships within families, but this particular relationship had seemed beyond repair.

I went to his funeral. Well, I was forced – my mum told me I had to. I couldn't give a shit about my dad, and I was angry with my mum for making me go. I remember just wanting to phlegm on his grave, which sounds hardcore, but it's true. Sometimes the truth is way too hardcore, and there we are. Either way, that was the end of it. That whole bad part of my life, all of that shit, was in a coffin with him. I suppose you should always look for closure in certain parts of your life, and that was mine.

The funeral coincided with the first date of Craig David's Following My Intuition tour, and following the success of our 'When the Bassline Drops' single, he'd invited me to be the main support act on each of the arena dates. I left my dad's funeral, got straight on my tour bus, and within hours

I was on stage performing to 15,000 people. I didn't see my house for over a month.

You're probably wondering about the grieving process. True, if I'd been close to him, I'd have been in bits – and my involvement in the tour would have been cancelled. But I genuinely believe that you can't grieve for a stranger, and my dad was a stranger to me.

I think of relationships in terms of them being an 'emotional bank account' between two people – a sort of spiritual joint account where one person or the other, or both people, keep depositing 'money' over the years. Every time you check on someone's well-being, you're making a deposit. Every time you put your pride to one side for the benefit of the other person, that's another deposit. Every birthday you're there for, every sacrifice you make, every little bit of tenderness and kindness, it all adds up. With a parent, maybe by the time a kid's 18, you've put a million quid's worth of emotional transactions into there, and if anything ever happened to you your kid would have a million emotions for you.

But if you've put nothing into that account, not even a tenner, and you've never nursed them, you've never let them sleep on your chest, you've never been there when they've really needed you, they'll have nothing for you when you die. If you've made a couple of small deposits but been so horrible that the account's basically in its overdraft, you're in real trouble.

So what have I actually taken from my relationship with my dad? Well, that's simple: he's a cunt, I'll never be like that, and my own legacy will be totally different.

On May 1st 2015 my daughter was born. I became a father, and, in that moment, when I saw my daughter, I really knew for the first time just how much of a cunt my dad had been. I think if your head's on straight, it's only when you become a parent that you can really understand just how much of a cunt you'd need to be to be a cunt to your own kids.

It's easy for an outsider to point out what's wrong with your own childhood, or say things like: 'You wouldn't want something that's happened to you to happen to your kid.' But sometimes people don't even see their childhoods as having been particularly bad, even if there's been some dark shit. They just thought their upbringing was *how it had to be*. Before I had a kid, I wasn't really that bothered about a lot of the stuff that had happened between me and my dad, or even about hard times I'd faced with my mum and brother. I wouldn't say I understood it, or why it had happened to me, but I didn't mind it, because it was all I knew. I just thought it was badman shit I had to cope with as best I could.

If that's ringing bells for you, know that in most situations things don't have to be a certain way and, in most situations, there are things you can do to improve life. But for me, that whole legacy of pain ended with my dad. I'll just take the small amount of good bits my dad did give me (and I'll delete the rest from my memory), then I'll throw in almost everything my mum taught me and, as for the rest … well, I'll make that up as I go along.

One thing I didn't expect about fatherhood was that almost overnight I found myself deciding, on the basis of precisely zero evidence, that everyone we passed in the street, everyone we met, and everyone who might cross our paths in any scenario, was almost certainly a fucking nonce.

After my daughter came along I found my protective instincts totally going into overdrive, and it took massive strength for me to overcome my phobia of other people so I didn't stunt her emotional health. I didn't like leaving her with anyone who wasn't either me or the missus, but I had to suck it up because I knew that as a parent your decisions have to be based on what's best for the child rather than whatever batshit notions are knocking around inside your head. So yeah, it's fair enough to have your eyes open for potential stranger danger, but you can't be calling the cops every time a nice old lady waves at your kid on the bus.

My son's still too young for this but one of the more positive qualities I've been trying to pass on to my daughter is the idea of independence and, with it, confidence. I noticed before we put her into nursery that she didn't always find it easy to socialise and I was upset that she was going into nursery so early – I wanted her to just be around us until she could talk and communicate properly. But I also saw that because of my lifestyle and how we live she's not always around loads of people, meaning that when she *was* around people she could seem antisocial and very clingy. She wasn't integrating well. This was a bit like my nonce problem: I was being overprotective. The irony was, it was my over-protectiveness that was standing in the way of my daughter being more sociable. It was sending me nuts but eventually I had to accept that I couldn't let my own personal fears hold her back from blossoming, and in the end she did go to nursery, she did integrate well with the other kids and she did develop more of her personality – it was the best thing ever for her.

I think I was probably so worried about how unsociable my daughter initially was because it was something I didn't recognise in myself and therefore had no way of knowing how to tackle, but sometimes the opposite is true, and having kids is like having a mirror held up in front of you. Take the whole concept of sharing: my daughter hasn't got her head around that yet. She won't share her toys; if her little brother touches one of them, she won't play with it any more, as if it's tainted. She is *not* happy about man touching her stuff. Seeing that streak coming out in my daughter is mad because I'm not a great sharer either, and I know that teaching her about sharing is going to involve teaching myself a few lessons too.

It'll be time well spent. On my *BDL Bipolar* album there's a song called 'Blood', which is all about my daughter's birth, and how things changed for me when she came along. In the song I'm speaking directly to her and there's a line where I promise that 'I'll spend money and time'. A lot of parents just throw money at problems, and they'll throw money at parenting, too, as if that's just another 'problem' that can be solved with a load of cash. I know that parenting technique all too well – it's the opposite of how my mum operated, but my dad would do it all the time. Don't get me wrong, I'm proud that I can put clothes on my kids' backs and food in their stomachs; but what's important for me and hopefully them too is that I want to know their favourite colour, their football team, their favourite song, the books they love to read. At the moment my daughter's favourite song is from the *Trolls* soundtrack; she likes to dance round the kitchen with me whenever it comes on. Those little things are priceless. As a father I just have to take them in and hope the memories never fade.

I just can't imagine missing out on seeing my kids growing up. As much as I think my dad's a cunt, I also know that at least in the early stages of my life he was around for me and my brother, along with those odd attempts to re-establish contact later on. Like, he wasn't *totally* absent. For better or worse, we at least knew who he was, but when I think about some of my other bredrin', they don't know their dads full stop; they only ever had a mum. I know there are all sorts of reasons for that: divorce; parents who pass away; mums who are definitely better off without certain men in their lives. And the result of that is that a lot of kids have to step up and be the man of the house when their dad's not around, meaning that they miss out on important parts of their own childhoods. So I know I'm lucky that I'm in a position to be around for my own kids.

That means making sure they have the right tools to live their lives by later on, but right now I'm determined that one of my biggest gifts to my own children – my only mission, right now – is to simply let them be children. I'd advise all new parents to remember that: don't force kids to grow up too quickly.

One perk of letting my own kids *be* kids is that my daughter doesn't yet have a sense that her dad has a job that's a bit different to your average job. When I'm out and about and someone asks me for a picture I'll always stand away from my family so they're not included – I might have made the decision to be in the public eye by making music, but my missus and my children didn't make that choice. That's why you'll notice it's all 'my missus' this and 'my daughter and son' that in this book. When they're older my kids can make the decision about being public figures themselves, if they want, but my job between now and until my son and daughter are of a decent age is to make their lives as normal as possible without being impacted by my fame.

Example: some celebrities dress their kids head to toe in designer clothes and wheel them out in front of the press.

My kids wear fucking Asda clothes. I had a big conversation with someone recently, and they said: 'If you can afford it, why wouldn't you buy Gucci and Ralph Lauren threads for your kids?' Ridiculous. My son's still at an age where he doesn't know if he's dressed in an egg carton or not, let alone what designer he's wearing, and my daughter couldn't give two shits about designer labels because she doesn't even know what they are. All she knows is that if she sees a muddy puddle she's going to play Peppa Pig and jump up and down in it until it's time to leave the park. You don't want to put your kid in the position of being told they can't jump in a puddle, just because they're the only kid at the playground in £1,000 trainers.

A similar thing happened after her third birthday party. She'd been given loads of presents, but once she'd emptied them all out of their boxes she left the toys in a pile, picked the biggest box she could find, grabbed her old dolly and two small balls and put them in the box, and played with that for the rest of the fucking day. Sure, a My Little Pony turned up in her imagined story at one point – and it was a My Little Pony she'd had for 18 months – but that was about as extravagant as it got. I could have just bought four quids' worth of cardboard boxes off Amazon and she'd have been none the wiser, and no less happy. It's like I was saying about trying to invent memories for your kids: you don't have control over it, and you just need to let kids go their own way.

Although it's true that everything about being a father is trial and error, you have to be trying to do your best. That's the most important thing, and it includes concepts like unconditional love, patience, willpower and selflessness. I'm not gonna lie, there have been moments when I've just wanted to leave the house and lie in a darkened room for five hours, but I never do, and even when babies are screaming I always put myself back in the room and make the best of a situation. You hear those stories, don't you, where they say: 'Oh, their dad said he was going to the shop for a pint of milk and a packet of Quavers, and he never came back.' And I'd be lying to you if I told you I'd never briefly considered that myself when it's all kicking off at home, but I soon snap out of it. I always go back and I always will.

Apart from the days and sometimes weeks when I've been away working, the toughest times I've experienced being a father have been down to knowing how and when to discipline my kids. I remember my dad's approach to discipline with me was ... not ideal. It'd go like this: he'd pull up in his car, get out, then go get a stool and a mad weightlifting belt out of the back of his car, and once I was bent over the stool he'd give me ten of the best. If I moved, or even flinched, he'd start again from ten. If he got to six and I fell off the bench, he'd start again. Then once he was done I'd have a bit of a cry and I'd sort myself, and then he'd take me on a DEEP shopping spree. A *fat* shopping spree. He'd take me to the West End for clothes, trainers, the whole lot, then he'd drop me back off at home.

You're probably thinking 'what the fuck' and, well, I did too. I'm not saying I was an angel when I was a kid; in fact, as I discuss elsewhere in this book, I was a scumbag a lot of the time, but I didn't learn anything from my dad's form of discipline. I was just confused. Why would he punish me, then buy me presents? Back then I didn't realise what was happening, but I've got a better idea now: he was losing control, then trying to say sorry – and in doing so he was trying to make himself feel better. Fucked up scenes for a number of reasons, but mainly because discipline should never be about losing control, and it should never be done through anger.

My take on discipline as a parent is that there has to be someone to say the fucking truth: 'What you're doing is wrong, and you shouldn't have done that.' And I believe that kids should be allowed to get things wrong, as long as they acknowledge the problem, understand why it's a problem and apologise where appropriate. I guess the tough part – and the problem my dad tried to solve when he took me shopping – is that there are times as a father when you have to be the father, not a friend. Same for any parent, I guess.

My mum often got the right balance. In our family she was always known as the strictest auntie, and all my cousins used to say: 'When you come to Tyrone's mum's house, she's militant.' But they would also say: 'Okay, so you might have to be in bed at nine o'clock sharp, but until then you'll have FUN. There'll be baking, play fighting, Connect 4, the whole lot.'

Even though my mum was strict, she let us have fun within her rules. If you abided by the rules and regulations, the world was your oyster; if you broke them them, your arse was grass. Every kid needs boundaries and routine. Think of it like this: you know your kid's a little shit, but you never discipline him. You never tell him he's wrong. You never force him to look at his action. Maybe it's because you don't want to make him sad, but what have you done long-term? Next thing you know he's a 26-year-old little shit, who's not so little any more, and he kicks and slaps harder. And now he's too big for a telling off from Dad. And then this big little shit gets thrown in the cage.

Now obviously, there's no foolproof way to make sure your kid's gonna grow up alright: plenty of children from broken homes with no love in their lives go on to have happy and stable adulthoods, while kids who grew up with a full family and a silver spoon shoved up their arse go off the rails and end up behind bars. Everyone and anyone can fuck up in their lives, but I guess what I want to be sure of is that if there ever comes a day when one of my kids is standing in front of me telling me that they've fucked up, I'll know that in no way can they say they fucked up because of me.

They won't have fucked up because they had a bad childhood – they'll have had the perfect childhood. They won't have fucked up because you didn't have the chance to get to university, or because of financial stress. My gran had 14 children, and of all of them only one bought their own house; my daughter and son are the first kids in my blood-line to grow up in a house that's been bought. So chances are, they'll just have fucked up because they're young, and that's what young people do. If they're honest with me and they know where they've gone wrong, and they know how to make sure they don't do it again, that's something I can live with all day every day. It'll just be up to them to brush themselves off, and go again. I will have given them enough life skills. The rest of it's on them.

Truth is, I just don't think I'd be able to cope if they grew up thinking of me the way I often thought of my own dad. Or if one day they were stood in front of me, having fucked up, telling me: 'It's because of you, you cunt.' It would destroy me.

My job is to show them the best avenues I possibly can, and to show them the right things in life, and show them stability. Words are cheap: don't think that just telling kids you love them is enough, because anyone can say those words. 'I love you' means a lot, but it's also the sort of thing we say so much that it ceases to have any meaning: it's just noise. Some of your job as a parent is what you say, but the most important part is in what you do: how you conduct yourself, how you talk to your missus in the house, whether or not you say please and thank you.

Some of that's very similar to what my dad taught me, but the difference with me is that I'll actually live by my own rules. I don't see myself as a good father. I just see myself as a father who tries. If I was to sit and tell you I know what I'm doing, I'd be lying. I'm just freestyling. But I do know that you cannot fake actions.

Love's something you talk about, but it's also something you show. If you show enough, you'll be good. I learned from my dad that the problem comes when you don't show any at all, and I'm determined to make sure that's something my own kids can never say about me.

5

SOCIETY: IT'S WHAT WE MAKE IT

In life, everybody needs to feel like they can fit in. We need groups of people around us who we feel comfortable with, and my idea of society is that all those groups of people can somehow exist alongside each other – and overlap, and help each other out – and form something bigger.

Society, for me, is all these people with mad differences but something in common: respect. People who can live side by side, even when there are people left right and centre trying to cause divisions.

A few years back I did this crazy documentary for the Noisey website, with a group of absolute Gs who called themselves the Knights of Skirbeck. I went up to Lincolnshire and in a small town called Boston I found a couple called Dave and Caroline. If you've ever met anyone called Dave or Caroline I don't need to describe my first impressions of Dave and Caroline: Dave seemed like a total Dave, Caroline was 100% a Caroline. But behind the front door of their unassuming new-build home, a whole new world opened up. Actually, it wasn't even behind the door. The first sign of what I was letting myself in for was the fact that their doorbell looked like a bat. (Vampire, not cricket.)

Turns out Dave and Caroline had a secret: at weekends they dressed up in proper old-school medieval gear and re-enacted old battles. Proper mad scenes: spears, shields, all these kindred spirits giving it the full 'yes m'lady, no m'lord'. That lot really fucking went for it. And I got into it as well, calling myself Sir Narstie, Lord of Bass. I just imagined I was in *Game of Thrones* and got stuck in. Dave and Caroline told me all about their passion: the fact they'd spent two grand on kit for their first weekend, and how people who lived nearby thought they were 'the local loonies'. But they were lovely people. After a bit of time with them, we hit the pub and I asked them and their mates whether they had many friends.

'Not really,' was the reply.

But this lot had found each other: other people who had the same interests. Dave and Caroline had found each other, and despite the fact that their bedroom was festooned with candles and bondage gear with a bed the shape of a coffin, they'd found other people on the same wavelength. Mates who'd look out for each other. They'd been quite lonely people, and hadn't ever quite fitted in, but through the Knights of Skirbeck they'd found their people. A lot of life is about finding your people.

For me, the worst thing for society is when the people who are supposed to move society forward are the ones creating the divisions; it's the ultimate betrayal.

When I was younger I had no idea who politicians were, and I didn't care. I'd see pictures of them in the paper or on the telly, in the news programmes, and, even though Westminster was only a few miles away from Brixton, I'd think to myself: 'That's a different Britain they're representing. Why would I feel any connection to that? How is it affecting me? I'm not seeing it in any way affecting my life.'

I saw oppression as being three circles, one within the other. You had the oppressed in the middle, then you had the police around them, doing the day-to-day, hands-on oppression, and then around that you had the politicians. The person giving the orders would be next to the people carrying out the orders, but for me as a young black boy, right in the middle of that centre circle, I felt like I was nowhere near the outer rings of the oppression. The only contact I had with the politicians was via the police. So, I thought: 'Fuck the politician. The politician's too far away from my oppression zone for me to care what they have to say, and they're so far away from me that they don't even know I exist.'

I mean, I was half right. It's not as if all the MPs were coming down to Brixton to see how we all were. But it wasn't until my late teens that I started to realise what was going on. There was a difference between how I felt those decisions were affecting my life, and how they actually *were* affecting my life. When I saw benefits to ill relatives being cut off even though they couldn't work, that affected my life. When I saw local community centres being shut down due to lack of funds, that affected my life. When I saw the police off on another stop-and-search mission, that was all affecting my life, and my family, and my community. It wasn't that politicians didn't know I existed. It was that they didn't fucking care.

Most young people don't vote because they think: 'What's the fucking point?' And I felt the same way – I didn't vote for ages, because I didn't think something I could do would make any difference. No wonder so many politicians wanted me to feel like I was nothing: they didn't want me to feel like I could change stuff. I decided that politicians were like prostitutes at the bar: they'll say all the nice things when they're trying to get the punter, and they'll tell you whatever they think you want to hear. I thought that at some point all their moral codes could be bought. I didn't vote at all during my twenties. I thought: 'They're all cunts; I can't vote for any of them.'

In more recent years I've come round to accepting the fact that while some of the biggest cunts imaginable are slouching around in the Houses of Parliament, some of the people on those leather benches are less cunty than others. More importantly, I'm up for accepting that if every young person who thought their vote didn't count actually *did* vote, the country would be in far better shape. You can't say democracy doesn't work if you don't follow through on your democratic right and actually vote. As I've said before, a quiet mouth doesn't eat. Next time there's an election or a referendum, get out there and put your cross in the box.

One of the things that changed my view and made me feel like I was being listened to was around the Brexit vote, when I got invited to Downing Street to sit down with MI5 and all their promotions companies. In the end I found myself going round London on a big bus (not *that* bus) with a load of MPs. A couple of them were alright, actually, although the main conversations I had went like this:

Me: 'Can I smoke on this bus?'

Them: 'Er, no.'

Anyway, the whole point of me being there wasn't to tell people which way to vote, just that they *should* vote. As a result, I'm proud to say I made the most young people vote in the last ten years. I never would have thought I'd have been proud to say I'd made people vote, especially when I didn't vote myself for so many years, but with time came a little bit of knowledge and acceptance of how things work. It comes down to this: if you know better, you should do better.

I still think there need to be more politicians who understand what's happening in my life, though. Like, I met the MP Jess Phillips when I was doing the *Great British Bake Off* – top woman, totally gets what life's like for people born without a plastic spoon in their mouth. But there aren't enough people with power in this country who really understand that life for a poor man is not about living; it's about surviving. And surviving isn't about big fat foreign holidays; it's about a new pair of trainers once a year being a real blessing.

The best posh person I ever met was Prince Charles – actually, I met him twice, and I spudded him both times. The first time was in Brixton (so at least some people from the outer circle head down to SW9) and the second was at an army shooting tournament. The spudding didn't go down that well second time round, truth be told – I just walked up to him and banged his hand, which got a little bit awkward, mainly because the security went to grab me. Turns out it's an offence to strike a member of the Royal Family, but I wasn't just going to bow and curtsy.

Anyway, I told him what I was doing at the army event (obviously, this was before I got kicked out of the cadets for robbing).

'Hello,' he said. 'Very interesting.'

The sort of thing you say when you haven't got a bloody clue what someone's just said to you but, fair fucks to the man, he didn't have me bundled into the back of a secret service van. I've got a lot of time for Prince Charles, actually; he's done a decent amount of stuff for poor kids. It was the Prince's Trust charity that funded my boy Dullah to get set up with all his music equipment, at a point when there was no way anyone's mum had a spare four-and-a-half grand for music equipment. Rent always had to come first.

That sort of outreach to disadvantaged people is well different to the sort of thing I saw from politicians when I was young. Even now, look at most of those MPs on TV and ask yourself if they know the feeling every poverty kid knows: when you get the Argos catalogue and you spend hours looking through all the toys, because that's the closest you're ever going to get to owning them. Ask them if they know how that kid's parents feel when they see their son with that Argos catalogue, knowing that they just won't be able to ever buy those toys for Christmas. Ask them how that parent feels when their kid opens their stocking on Christmas morning and finds six bits from Poundland, and thinks: 'My friends get more than this. Does that mean I've been bad?' Ask them how that idea of being 'bad' is so relentless and shit that it becomes a reality and leads to transgression and crime and prison.

MPs don't have to worry about that. Their kids don't have to be worried about getting nicked for carrying a little bit of weed. Why *would* they worry? Daddy knows a good lawyer. So it's no wonder that politicians are so often responsible for driving a wedge between the people in this country.

That's how you end up with a tragedy like Grenfell. It was one of the most fucked up things I've ever seen. Young people with their whole lives ahead of them, losing their lives because of corporate greed, and politicians looking the other way. Except it wasn't just young people in that building: it was parents, grandparents and great-grandparents.

It could have been my mum. It could have been my grandma. Black people, white people, Greek people, Turkish people: they all died in that building and they were all human beings.

I remember the day after Grenfell burned; I'd just come off tour, and I knew there were still boxes of T-shirts and hoodies off the merch stand in the back of my car. I was only half an hour away so I headed over to west London to hand them out to anyone who needed something to wear, make a donation to the fund and see if I could be useful. I helped hand out water and clothes to people who'd just seen their lives go up in flames.

When someone dies you don't always know what to say, but sometimes being there's enough, and I wanted to be there for Grenfell. When man's grieving, sometimes you don't need to say anything and your company is some small kind of comfort. What was I supposed to say to those people? If your mum just burned in that building on the 24th floor, what could someone really say to you? So all I did was hang out, chat if people wanted to, and hope that people could feel my energy: 'Man's just here for you, innit. If you want to vent, scream, whatever, I'm here.'

I can vouch for what I saw with my own two eyes: during my time at Grenfell, I saw local groups coming together and people from all over London coming to help. I saw the local community bringing thousands of pounds' worth of food and water. I saw hundreds of people who wanted to help. It was society coming together in a time of need. But in my time there, I didn't see a single politician. You see the true person in the moment when they react, not in what they say afterwards. In any crisis situation your first intention is your natural intention, and your natural intention is your honest one. What does it say that a politician's first intention is to stay away?

The tragedy of Grenfell isn't just about what happened that night in June 2017. It's about the years and decades of neglect that led up to it, as well as what happened in the days, weeks and years afterwards. Tower blocks around the country continue to be unsafe for the people who live in them. Thousands of lives are still at risk. And nobody's in prison over Grenfell, of course. In the months that followed, nobody was held accountable, while kids who shoplifted because they didn't have any food continued to get seven months in prison, and a mum travelling to their third job of the night continued to get court orders because they forgot to tap in on the bus.

When politicians' actions are so brazen that even a fucking idiot can see what's going on, what's their excuse? Yet still politicians wonder why young people, and black people, and working class people in this country are angry. If you're angry now, that's another sign that you should vote, or do something to make your voice heard.

I saw anger come to a head during the London riots of 2011, after the police gunned down a guy called Mark

Duggan. Those riots – all across London, north to south, over three days – were rebellion. People love to think they're better than animals, but we're not, and the looting showed you that when you push an animal into a corner, to its breaking point, it goes into survival mode. Fight or flight. At that particular time, people decided to fight.

I was out in Brixton during those riots. I was on the roads: I saw places burning. Absolute madness. I remember walking down Ferndale Road minding my own business, and from one end I saw bare riot police walking up towards me. All of a sudden, out of nowhere, dozens of Yardies appeared with machetes. The police started to run. I literally saw the riot police throw down their shields and *leg it*. You know things are out of control when the riot cops are running away.

There's only one authority rioters will respect in that sort of situation. I went up to north London later on in the riots, and I saw this Yardie woman looking for her son. Then I saw her find him, strolling down the fucking street with a looted flat-screen telly! And then I saw her do something the riot police would never have managed: she battered him, got him to leave the telly in the street, and marched him home!

I can't say I'm surprised by the lack of respect young poor, working class and black kids show the police. Growing up, I saw first-hand the impact of the very worst of police racism and in fact the only racism I directly encountered was from the police. Even though the Brixton I knew was a black area, the entire police force seemed to be white, and every person had a bad story about a policeman who abused their power.

Think about this situation: me and you are standing outside the shop. We see a group of boys walking down to the shop kicking a football. Then we see an unmarked police car pull up, and the cops jump out and stop the kids. And they start searching them down. Why? No reason, or at least not any reason the Met would want to admit to. Me and you have clearly seen that the kids have been victimised and we have a choice. Maybe we're worried that if we step in, we'll end up in the cells ourselves, so we don't say anything, we mind our own business, we turn a blind eye, and we let nature take its course. But what happens then? Those youths now can't stand the feds. They've been turned. And they'll remember that when they were being searched down, there were people standing there who did nothing. So when they see something like that happen to someone else, they'll also turn a blind eye. It's a never-ending cycle.

One event that sticks with me came when I was nine years old and I was playing knock down ginger a few streets away, even though my mum had told me to stay in the house. But I'd sneaked out anyway to go and play. We hit a house but it turned out to be where a policeman lived – something I only realised when he came out in his uniform. I was running off but he caught me, and he punched me in the stomach. And then he said to me: 'If you ever fucking come to my house again, you little black shit, I will fucking do you.'

I couldn't tell my mum because I'd sneaked out of the house, so that was that. Now I'm older, I look back and wonder what would have happened – what *could* have happened – if I'd told her. If she'd gone to the police station to complain, would they have believed her? Actually, the fucked up thing is that's not even the question. The real issue is that, yeah, they probably would have believed her. They'd totally have believed that one of their officers hit a kid and called him a little black shit. And they'd have done nothing about it.

But that was the level of power they had back then – and like I say, everyone had a similar story. All of that leads to a never-ending spiral between street kids and the police – it's a catch-22 because of course nothing will change when no black man is ever going to want to grow up to be a policeman. And I've seen with my own eyes that even when black men and women do join the police force, most of them end up as fucking coconuts. For the police system to change you have to get police officers who truly represent each and every part of the communities they're supposed to service. Otherwise you'll end up with a load of rich kids with batons and guns policing the streets, and nothing will ever change.

I know not all white people are racist. I think it's a mistake to assume that just because someone doesn't know much about a culture, that means they reject or hate it. And yeah, we all know there's cunts, but some people aren't cunts. About ten years ago I went to Sunderland, up near Newcastle, while I was on tour with Tim Westwood. Now I don't know if you've spent much time in Sunderland but it's just under 95% white, and black people make up less than 1% of the population. And I was in this cab with Westwood when the taxi driver said, out of the blue, that he'd never seen a black person face to face. To me, this guy who'd grown up in Brixton, this was totally flabbergasting. This geezer had *never met a black person before.*

Thing is, you could say that him coming out with it for no reason was insensitive or whatever, but we got talking with him and this fella was just a decent guy. He wasn't racist; he simply lived in deepest darkest Sunderland where there just weren't loads of black people casually walking around listening to reggae and jerking chicken. And yeah, maybe he lived in a bubble, but I'd grown up in my own bubble in Brixton, too, where as far as I was concerned it was a black community and every sweet shop was black-owned. I'd come up in that community thinking that the rest of the world was like Brixton, thinking that in every shop you could buy a fried dumpling.

So how did I respond to the cab driver telling me what he did? Well, there might have been a few options. 'How dare you bring that up': that'd have been one. And true, not every black person wants to get in a cab and start talking about ethnicity any more than every white person wants to get in a cab and talk about their favourite Taylor Swift song. But I didn't mind. 'Why haven't you tried to integrate with black people?' – that would have been another more aggressive way of taking the conversation. But instead we just chatted.

As the Christmas tree air fresheners swung from his rear-view mirror, I talked to him about Brixton and he talked to me about Sunderland. Instead of a confrontation, we had a conversation, and I reckon we both came out of that short cab ride better people. In situations like that, sometimes a chat is the best thing.

Similar thing: people sometimes ask me why I go on *Good Morning Britain* and chat with Piers Morgan and his mates. But when I go on morning telly and represent myself, and let a million ITV viewers know I'm a fun guy who's turned things round, it's not just about me. It's about people like that Sunderland cab driver who might never see another black person seeing me without it always coming down to the stereotypical ideas they might have about black people. It wasn't so long ago that whenever you'd see a black person on morning TV it would be for a negative reason in a news bulletin.

I would rather be there with Piers Morgan and be a jester for 20 minutes, and show my people in a whole different light, than for the only black face on the show to be one linked with knife crime or gun crime. Everything in life comes with a price and that's a price I'm more than happy to pay.

That said, I'm not going to try to find a 'middle ground' or 'have a chat' with an EDL member, because talking to people who don't want to listen is a waste of oxygen, but the more time I spend outside Brixton in different communities of people who on the face of it have little in common, the more I realise how similar so many of us are.

I'm black and I'm fat; you might be skinny and white. I might smoke weed (spoiler: I do smoke weed) and you might not smoke weed. Whatever our differences we probably both like a burger, or we might both like sex. (Spoiler 2: I also like sex.) (And burgers.) Point is, we might not tick every single box on each other's lists, but in some boxes we'll match up, and that's where our common ground is. Instead of concentrating on the things we don't agree on, let's think about the things we do agree on. We might have different backgrounds, different cultures and different religions, but more often than not we have surprisingly similar dreams, we all have families we want to support, we all laugh and cry and bleed when we're cut.

And we all get ill. Living in the UK, the NHS is something we've had for so long that we sometimes take it for granted, to the point where it's easy to slip into the trap of complaining when we have to wait a bit longer in the doctor's surgery for our appointment, or longer than we expected for an operation. But let me tell you a story from a few years back that I always think of when people complain about the NHS.

So when I was really little, I was lucky enough to get the opportunity to visit extended family members in Jamaica, and my grandad's house had a big porch area between the door and his front gate. Jamaica's big for stray dogs and in that porch area were about twenty wild dogs that my grandad had made a little bit less wild – the only catch was they'd only listen to him. And this is Jamaica, so of course these dogs are off their fucking heads and carrying all sorts of diseases. Total savage mutts. And so my grandad had to escort you from the front door to the front gate, or this pack of dogs would attack you, but in the haste of a sunny day my grandma told my cousin Jermaine to run to the ice cream van, forgetting about the dogs, and of course he ran off, the dogs attacked him and we had to take him to hospital. And on the way to the nearest hospital, we saw a guy lying in a wheelbarrow.

Now I don't really need to state that this guy in the wheelbarrow was not in a good way. After the age of eight none of us can ever expect to find ourselves in a wheelbarrow for a good reason. As we got closer, we saw that he had a gunshot wound in his stomach. This bro, dumped by someone by the side of the road in a fucking wheelbarrow, was bleeding out of his gut and screaming in agony in the beating midday sun. Our cab driver just kept on driving straight past him. This was the sort of thing he saw every day: someone dying by the side of the road, not able to get any help from doctors because he didn't have any medical insurance.

Cars were driving past; people were walking past. *We* were driving past, with our red passports and our holiday insurance. But this guy was curled up and fucked because he was poor. That's why the NHS is important.

Or let's bring this closer to home. Imagine there's another car driving down the road in the UK on its way to some posh event. In the back you've got Ed Sheeran, Bill Gates, the guy who invented Amazon, the queen and Madonna. And let's say it's a big car, so there's room for you too. Put together the wealth of everyone else in that car and you've probably got enough money to buy five countries outright. But then there's a car crash. Glass and metal everywhere, limbs everywhere, blood everywhere, Ed's guitar's scratched, the queen's crown's fallen off; everything's fucked up. And while everyone's crawling out of the car and lying in pools of their own blood, nobody knows these people are Ed, Bill, Amazon bloke, Madonna and the queen, and they don't know you're you either. All anyone sees is a group of seriously hurt people lying on the floor, covered in blood, who need help. They need adrenaline, morphine, resuscitation, help.

And I know you're probably thinking: 'What about the driver? How is he absent from this scenario? Am I supposed to deduce that the driver escaped unhurt and extrapolate that the driver might have been in on this? Did the driver crash the car intentionally as part of a conspiracy?' Bruv, stop thinking about the driver and think about this: in the moment of life or death, it doesn't matter how famous the passengers are or how rich they are because in that instant all they need is help. They're just humans who've been fucked up. And here in the UK, every one of those humans – rich or poor – would get instant treatment. That's the importance of the NHS.

There are some total Gs working there as well. There was this time back in the day when I basically nearly lost my hand – I'd been attacked by a crackhead and in the carnage of him trying to fuck me up and me trying to get away from him, I'd cut my hand on one of his teeth. Afterwards I started getting gangrene, which then – boom – went into full-on septicaemia. It had only been a small cut, but what I didn't know was that anyone's mouth is mad infected, and a crackhead's mouth is likely to be an even more dangerous place. My hand started getting red. *Really* red. And the pain – I swear down, I smoked four and a half ounces of weed, then ran out of weed, and it was only when I'd finished all the weed that the pain really came through. I was in the studio spitting over some beat or other and then, just like that, the tip of my finger just dropped off on the floor. Blood was just pouring out of my hand on to the floor. The pain was diabolical. At that point I thought: 'Hm, I think I should go to the hospital.'

The doctor couldn't believe it. He said: 'How have you possibly managed to suppress this pain for so long?'

I said: 'Bruv, I've smoked four and a half ounces of weed.'

He went: 'I shouldn't be telling you this, but that's the best thing you could have done.'

Teachable moments from this? Smoke weed for pain? Don't get fucked up by crackheads? Listen to your body when it's screaming out for attention? Hard to say really, but big up that NHS doctor for reinforcing my belief that sometimes weed is the best medicine. (Medical note: weed in this instance was actually the second best medicine and is not a substitute for a tetanus jab in your arse.)

When I hear about politicians wanting to scrap the NHS or sell bits of it off to whoever's got the biggest chequebook, it makes me sick. And yeah, this is partly because I saw my mum working in the NHS, heard her stories about the poor funding and saw with my own eyes the long hours she and her colleagues were working, but I want to make sure the NHS is cool and that my kids' generation and their own kids grow up with the privilege of knowing that while the cards might be stacked against them in so many other parts of their lives, they're never going to die in a fucking wheelbarrow just because of their bank balance.

Obviously the fact that the NHS, one of the best things about Britain, has been held together for decades by immigrants and the children of immigrants, makes 52% of the voter's attitude towards immigration all the more mad. I mean, I know some people who voted in the 2016 Brexit vote will tell you it's about fucking 'sovereignty' or 'blue passports' or whatever, but it's not as if they were pro-immigration, right?

I won't say the result of the Brexit vote exactly surprised me, but I was shocked that after having spent most of my life seeing the United Kingdom gradually taking a one step back, two steps forward approach to becoming more united, I witnessed about a hundred steps back being taken overnight. Any progress with integration that had been made in my lifetime seemed to have been shat on.

Now I might be biased here because I'm the grandson of immigrants, and also because I'm not a cunt, but I'm going to say that immigration's no bad thing.

The fact that you're reading this book in the first place makes me think you're probably with me on this. But does it help to see the other side's perspective? Again, I'm a bit wary of the whole 'let's bring society together by agreeing to find a middle ground' argument because firstly there isn't a fucking middle ground when it comes to racism – you're either not racist, or you're a shithead. And secondly, because racists are never interested in 'hearing the other side', are they? But let's for a moment take a break from our normal thinking, right, and go for a walk in other people's shoes.

And if you're the sort of person who never leaves London, that's going to mean taking a walk outside the M25. London feels like the most multicultural place in Britain, but it's a mistake to think that everywhere is like London. I mean, why do you think everyone in London was shocked by Brexit? It's because they thought London was the same as Britain, but it's not. Think about places like Sunderland, with my mate driving his minicab, or Six Mile Bottom or fucking Leatherhead. After you get past cities, it's traditional England. It's rural, it's farming, it's fights outside Pizza Express. You don't even need to go that far: drive half an hour in any direction out of any major city and you'll find that people have found their communities changing.

The reason London doesn't have a problem with the integration of the Polish, Turkish, Jamaicans or Africans is that it's been integrated the right way. But if you go to a place like Falmouth or Oxford, or somewhere that still has cobbled streets and Victorian buildings and police stations that close at 6pm, and then influx them with 700 eastern Europeans, then tell the residents they won't get a council flat and that they don't have a job any more, what do you expect to happen? Like, do you think everyone's going to roll out the red carpet? Are you okay in the head? So I do understand why people in those areas are opposed to immigration: there's no integration. They've lived one way for years, and now they feel as if their way of living has suddenly changed. But here's the thing: the ethics of 'keep Britain white' have meant that for some people, integration won't ever happen.

I wonder how I'd feel about if the same thing was happening to Jamaica. What if one day high class white English people decided to take over Jamaica and take all their natural resources? I mean, that's literally what happened back in the day and I can tell you how I feel about it: not very good.

Hear this: it's all about teachings. Every man or woman was a child once, and, before that, they were a blank page. It's the teachings we receive that make us prejudiced: nobody's born racist, or homophobic, or misogynistic. It's something we're taught. Anyway, cultures are mixing. Ten years ago your normal racist white boy wanted to wear shoes and a shirt and look sophisticated. Nowadays he's wearing Yeezys. And just look at the way drill music has infiltrated posh white neighbourhoods: a pouch on their waist, a Nike glove with their tracksuits. That's culture changing, integrating, being more accepting. By the same token I'm on a renaissance mission at the moment: I love Winston Churchill, the Kray twins, old English history. I'm down for all that because that's my culture as well.

But let's be honest. A lot of the reason people who see themselves as 'traditional English' don't like immigrants is that immigrants make a lot of English people feel ashamed of themselves. Sorry, but that's the God's honest truth. The country was based on the raiding and pillaging of other countries and there's a naturally inherited sense of laziness. Don't forget my grandparents, part of the Windrush gener-ation after World War II, came over to work and were only invited to do so because English people didn't want to do jobs they thought were beneath them. My grandmother's

80 now but she was 20 when she came to the UK and took a low-paying job as a nurse, because none of the existing Londoners wanted to wipe arses all day. Same with her mates who worked in construction, on buses, the whole lot: these people helped rebuild the country after the war.

The simple truth then was the same as the simple truth now – the majority of immigrants show up how lazy and greedy and entitled some people can be. They hold up a mirror that some people just don't want to look in.

Thing is, in any society there are going to be different cultures bumping into each other every day. And I guess they all have different values: for instance, most English culture looks at people who smoke weed as dossers. If you sit in your house on a Friday night smoking puff, you're a waste of space. But a guy who does cocaine after a hard day's roofing: well, he's a hard-working labourer, and it's absolutely fine that he and his mates are going to get smashed in the pub after work with a little half a gram. And again: smoking weed is frowned upon, while drinking alcohol is celebrated.

My point is that these preconceptions aren't going to do anyone any favours. In reality there's no such thing as normal. What's normal to me isn't normal to you. You might be a standard traditional white man, while I'm a standard traditional black man: I grew up in the teachings of Rastafari and church with a Caribbean background – sleep on Saturday, rice and peas on Sunday, the whole thing. That might not be normal to you, but your life might not seem normal to me. So if we both think we're normal, and neither of us thinks the other one is normal, where does that get us?

The trick's not to think of 'normal' and 'not normal'. The trick is to recognise that people are different, and the test of whether you can operate within a society is to ask yourself what judgements you make based on that difference. If you're not making any judgements at all, you're on the right track.

6

WORK: WHY TO DO IT, HOW YOU GET IT, AND HOW TO KEEP IT

If you ever wonder why you're at a stationary place in life or why you're not getting any further, you need to ask yourself why the opportunities aren't coming to you. Are you on the radar of opportunity? Are you even on the same frequency? And then you need to ask yourself about the very nature of opportunity.

Me, I learned early on that opportunity isn't just going to knock on your door. This bizarre concept called opportunity won't randomly miss out five million other people and come straight to you and say: 'Fuck Pete, Tom and Andy down the road, *you* should get a break.' It doesn't work like that, and nine times out of ten you have to go TO opportunity.

And I figured that out because I'd also learned at an early age – with some dismay – that it would be necessary for me to get off my arse. My first money-making scheme: washing's people's cars when I was seven years old. I filled a bucket with water, threw in some of my mum's Fairy Liquid, and rummaged around in the box everyone has under their sink (you know the one; it contains polish for shoes that have long been thrown out, in a tin so old that the price label has the old Co-Op logo on it) until I found a sponge. Then I walked up and down the street, knocking on doors.

My pricing scheme (£3 for one car, £6 for two) wasn't exactly sophisticated, but at least it was transparent. Not that everyone on my street even had one car, let alone two, but still.

I quickly realised that most people didn't want their car washed by some kid with a bucket of washing-up liquid, nothing to rinse it off with, and a sponge that was probably last used to clean a toilet, especially if the last time they saw that kid he'd been vaulting over the fence in their back garden on his way to or from some local mischief, but some people did say yes, and I started to notice a pattern. Phrases like 'excuse me' and 'thank you' were more likely to get a yes, and maybe even an extra 50p thrown in as a tip. My mum had brought me up to know that manners were important, but this was the point when I realised manners weren't just for other people's benefit: they could make you money, too.

The sort of household you grow up in will have a big impact on how your approach work and what you want to get out of it. For instance, a difference I've noticed between Jamaicans and Africans is that with Jamaicans there's an instant feeling that they want to go straight into hard work, whereas with African people they're brought up thinking more of education. So where Caribbean families just want you to not be a dosser, and the idea is that any job is better than no job, African families want all their children to be lawyers and barristers, and are really trying to push the educational factor. A lot of Jamaican people I know started working at 16 and just grabbed any job they could find. Plenty of them found a decent trade, but they never really studied, and in loads of cases that meant they could never really go for their dreams.

To me, that's the difference between *hard work* and *smart work*. They're both work, and when you're 19 it might not seem like there's much of a difference, but as you get older and your career either takes off or stays where it is the difference becomes more obvious. Two people might both start off on minimum wage when they're 18 years old – but fast forward two decades and one of them will still be on minimum wage, while the other's worked their way up the ladder to be on £40k.

So this is where I think parents have a responsibility to show their kids that there can be something noble about hard work. I reckon most parents want their kids to be attached to their legacies somehow, but if kids don't see parents working hard, how can they respect the very notion of a bit of graft? You can't respect something you don't know.

Between the ages of 11 and whenever it is we finish our education, we're told that the rest of our lives will be defined by the qualifications we get in our GCSEs, our A levels and everything else. Real talk, though: qualifications don't mean shit if you can't sell yourself, and while I haven't got many certificates for academic achievement, I've always had an A★ in self-confidence.

There's a point at school when you get sent off to see the careers advisor. Successful people and celebrities usually tell big stories about the time they went to their careers advisors – it'll usually be something like: 'They laughed when I said I wanted to be a singer / actor / YouTuber / voted out in week three of *Big Brother* in one of the series after it moved to Channel 5. They laughed then but look at me now!'

Actually, I have a bit of sympathy for these men and women who sit around in schools trying to figure out some way kids can make a bit of money when they're older. I mean, first off none of these advisors sat in a similar room 25 years ago and told an adult that they wanted to be a careers advisor, so it must be gutting to hear a load of kids reeling off their hopes and dreams.

Also, truth is that for every kid who's laughed at for wanting to be a successful actor or singer then goes on to make it, there's a thousand who really will never make it. You don't hear stories in autobiographies from people going: 'My careers advisor laughed at me when I said I wanted to be the next Tom Cruise, but I didn't listen! Turns out I'm a twat and my careers advisor had a good point, because now I'm stacking shelves in a supermarket.' You don't even get those autobiographies in the first place. So I understand how if you're a careers teacher, and the thirtieth person that day is coming in saying they want to make a living in esports or by winning *The X Factor*, you might want to say: 'Hm, how about a Plan B?'

But that's why it comes back to confidence. I was expecting to get laughed out of the room when I told my careers advisor I wanted to be a bomb disposal expert, but I explained my reasons with such confidence that he replied: 'That's actually a really interesting idea.'

Confidence is the difference between been bold and being meek. There are loads of talented people around with no confidence and they're the ones seeing missed opportunities (or maybe not even realising there were opportunities in the first place). But the guys who get all those missed opportunities? More often than not, they're the ones with less talent but plenty of attitude.

The way you communicate with people, and how you let people talk to you, defines how seriously you're taken in life, and if there's no passion in your encounters with other people you're fucked. In the world of work you're the seller – and the product is yourself.

A lot of people are scared by work situations but I see life no different to pulling chicks. Fellas, look at it this way – are you telling me that, with every girl you ever said hello to, it was as simple as her saying hello back and that three minutes later she was sucking your cock? No fucking way. Out of ten women maybe only three will suck your cock. In the interests of gender equality, it'd have been good here to propose a similar situation if you're a woman but unfortunately my argument collapses due to the fact that men can't control themselves and won't ever turn down sex, because we're all dogs, but I hope you see my point: you can't think that everyone you speak to in life is going to say yes to everything you want.

The truth is this: you really don't need to be amazing at something for it to seem like you're good at it. You just need to be competent enough not to fuck it up. Sure, being amazing gets you in the Top 20% of whatever area you're in, but you can still get in the Top 30% by adhering to the basics – being competent, turning up on time, and not punching your boss or photocopying your ballsack at the Christmas party. There are thousands of business management 'gurus' knocking around who'll happily charge you three grand for a course on how to get ahead in cut-throat industries, but here's my three-step guide to all you really need to know:

1. Be good.
2. Be reliable.
3. Don't be a fucking dick.

My first (and I suppose only) real job was a spell working at the 3 Monkeys Indian restaurant in Herne Hill, which is one stop up from Brixton and a little bit posher, although that didn't mean the clientele weren't just as rowdy as in anywhere on Acre Lane.

How was it, working at 3 Monkeys? Absolutely shit, thanks for asking: I'd get there at 5pm, after I'd finished at college, and I'd work until kicking out time. When I say 'kicking out time', I mean people were totally turfed out of the place, and that was particularly true on Friday nights. As you know, I spent a lot of my younger days hanging around nightclubs with my dad, so I'd seen pissed people before, but none of that had prepared me for quite how off their faces people get at an Indian restaurant. Always the middle class ones, too – unwinding after a difficult week. ('Unwinding' here means banging about eight Stellas, shouting at every waiter in the place, then spilling half your korma on the table and most of the rest down the loosened tie that'll probably be fastened round your head by the time you're turned away at the door at Inferno's on Clapham High Street.)

I spent most of my time in the kitchen, though, and if you've ever ordered a takeaway and wondered whose job it is to put the little cardboard lids on the foil containers, I regret to inform you that the answer is that it's probably someone like a teenage Big Narstie, getting paid £180 for a month's work. I know when people talk about their younger days they usually go, 'Oh obviously back then a hundred and eighty pounds was a lot of money, back then you could buy a house with seven pounds fifty and have change left over for a Twix', but £45 a week is shit now and was shit then.

The turning point for me came when I had a chat with Michael, who was the leader of a youth centre that ran up the road in Stockwell. The 409 Project had been set up to try to help out teenage kids like me who'd either offended or were likely to. I think he must have taken a bit of a shine to me. I remember one day he said to me: 'What do you want to do?'

'I'm just from road, innit?' I replied. I kind of knew how my life was mapped out. There'd be crime, there'd be unfortunate incidents and, like my teacher told me, I'd be behind bars or in the ground before my twenties were over. What I *wanted* to do wasn't something I ever really thought about – I didn't feel like I had a choice.

Michael was having none of that. 'You're a black king,' he told me. 'You can do more than all this. You can be a businessman; you can have an office.'

And obviously I just went: 'Don't be stupid, I'm never going to have an office.'

He replied: 'What do you mean? I'm going to give you an office.'

And that was that. He paid me to go to the houses of other kids and to talk with them, like a caseworker on the youth offending team, and yes, he gave me an office. It was just a chair and a table in a room, and thinking about it now I reckon the room might actually have been a broom cupboard, but that didn't matter. I can still picture the tiny desk with a phone on it – not much, but that little room was everything to me.

The first thing I did when I sat down was phone my mum and say: 'I'm working! I've got a job and a desk.'

Sometimes I just used to sit at that desk and think: 'Man's fifteen years old, and he's got an office.' I started thinking about myself differently at that point. Before that, I'd never have been able to imagine myself in an office. 'I don't wear a suit! I'm not going to the bank! I'm just a ghetto kid!' But Michael's generosity opened my mind to a lot of things.

Not many people can believe without seeing, and until I eventually found myself in an office sitting behind a desk, I didn't think I could do it. My mentality had created a wall that was ten feet high, but as soon as I saw my office, the wall seemed so low that I could simply step over it. That little desk changed my life.

In theory Michael was my first boss, but it wasn't until later on that I realised he wasn't only that: more importantly, he was a mentor. There are times in life when it feels like we're hanging on by our fingertips but if you're lucky, like I was, you'll find someone who extends their hand and helps pull you up. It might not be the person you expect and to start with you might not even know you need their help, but don't push it away when the time comes. It could change your life, just like Michael changed mine.

Whether it's washing cars for £3 a pop, helping out troubled teens while being a troubled teen myself, or performing to thousands of people for considerably more, I've found that working for your money is 100% good for self-esteem.

People don't talk about that so much, do they? Sure, they'll say jobs are good for money so you can pay your rent, and they'll say it's important when it comes to impressing the sort of people who are impressed by money, but too little's said about how honest work can turn around the way you think about yourself.

Now, don't get me wrong – I know there are plenty of people who are desperate to work and just can't catch a break. Unemployment's a fucker and it's only the very luckiest among us who'll never experience it. But if you're *able* to work and there's a job somewhere with your name on it, don't reject it out of laziness. I've seen bare laziness in my bredrin' and, truth is, if you've got nothing to do you'll easily get depressed and bored. Sitting in your flat for weeks on end does strange things to your mind. Human beings are social animals – if you're secluded and not interacting with society it'll affect your mental state. You need to communicate, and interact. And you need to feel like you're doing something with your life.

Now, maybe you got good grades at school. Maybe you've got a super-impressive CV made of gold leaf. Maybe you're just mega-rich and your dad plays lacrosse with the boss of some Forbes 100 company, who'll give you a starting salary of £80k. If you're any of those people, all power to you: your career is yours to fuck up. So don't fuck it up.

But if you're none of those people, you need to get clever. Whether it's JP Morgan or JD Sports, the first thing is you need to look the part. I'm going to say it again: seeing is believing. And the first hurdle to securing the bag is always how you look. If you leave your house looking like total shit, why would I give you £100 to change your life? Nobody likes desperate; desperate is not sexy. Let me tell you a secret: when I've been at my poorest, *that's* when I've worn all my jewellery. And that's when opportunity has always come knocking.

I've seen this story so many times in the music industry. You've got a snappy dresser, who's a flash talker, turning up to a meeting in a leased car. He's skint, but he's a chancer, and if you compare that with a millionaire who arrives at a meeting on the bus, you *know* which one's going to get 15 acts signed to their record label. You'll always need to walk the walk eventually, but sometimes talking the talk is a good first step. And what's true in the music industry is true in so many other areas of life. Whatever sort of work you do, chances are an Armani suit and some flash words will get you twice as much work. (This does not apply to astronauts.) Being able to bluff and blag in any situation is a positive thing: a smart shirt and some smart shoes, and you're halfway there. It's about who you are in the moment, rather than who you were yesterday.

Of course, as someone who now has to find the right people to work with and make sure they're the best choice for every role, I have to remember my own tricks and make sure they're not used against me! If some geezer turns up in a flash motor and does some smooth talking, I have to remember not to fall for it all myself. Truth be told, the most important people you'll meet – not in terms of how powerful they are, but in terms of what they'll do for your personal development – might well look beyond all the shit they see in front of them, and they'll try to find out what you really have to offer. That's what I try to do with people I'll work alongside, just as Michael did all those years ago when he gave me that desk.

Once you've got a job, the next step is to actually keep it. This means going out and getting obliterated no more than four times a week, and making sure you're in bed before 2am on a school night. One of the toughest things to get your head around is the fact that it's someone else's job to be in charge of what you do. Often the most power hungry are those who never had any power before: the classic traffic warden situation. All of a sudden they have control over people's lives and destinies, but if they're not in a good place themselves and if they don't love themselves, they fuck people up.

My advice, if your boss is being a dick for no reason, is to check the situation you're in: your inclination might be to call him a cunt or chuck his briefcase in a skip but real talk, sometimes it's alright to lose the battle to win the war. Remember, as much as human beings like to think they're better than animals, we still act like them, and if you're the lowest on the food chain you have to be man enough to respect that rank.

You also need to know you can change that rank. Asking for a promotion, for instance, is never going to be easy. There are a couple of options if you reckon you deserve more cash, more prestige, or a better job title.

Plan A is just to work really hard, cross your fingers that the right people are going to notice, and wait for the new job to roll in. Plan B is to wait until your boss uses the toilet, walk in there, whack their head off the sink and say: 'I want more money, you dirty little slag.' I'd say Plan B is probably best avoided, and like I always say: men lie, women lie, numbers don't. If man's smashing the numbers you don't *need* to ask for a promotion; it's offered to you on a plate. If you want to change your position in the food chain, anything's possible, but the only way you get everything to fall into place is to add to your worth. Little steps at a time, that's all it takes. Start off like an ant, work up to being a meerkat.

Don't want to be a meerkat? You know what, that's fine too. If you're happy working the trolleys at Asda, don't feel as if you have to break out of what's right for you. Not everybody is ruled by dreams of greatness; not everybody wants or needs to sit in a palace. You could get a job cleaning raves at four o'clock in the morning for two years, and that gives you all the money you need, and that's fine. It's natural to me to have a hundred grand and to want to turn it into a million, while there are other guys who've come from nothing, just like me, and they'd see a hundred grand

and see it as a hundred quid a week, every week, for the next 20 years.

And there's nothing wrong with that, if it's what you want. If you're paying your rent, buying food, taking a holiday once a year and are happy with your life, that's fine: there's nothing wrong as long as you're true to yourself and you're comfortable with that.

The problem only comes if you know deep down that you're not comfortable with that lifestyle. Sadness thrives in the space between dreams and reality. Any person who doesn't want to go for dreams because they're comfortable how they are, you can't criticise them: they've already won. Being content with a simple job is a dream in itself: you turn up, you do your job, you fuck off home and you have a nice life. That's more rewarding than scurrying around chasing some dream – often, a dream that society and the media have invented for you. I know many people who have acceptance of comfortability – and there are plenty of people in my family just like that. Their lives are full of love and joy, and very little stress.

And listen, you can drive yourself mad chasing a life-style. No matter how good a job you have, someone will always have a better one. No matter how big your salary is, someone else will always earn more. Got a company car? Julian over there has got a private jet. And no matter how hard you work to get to the top, someone will *always* have a bigger private jet. You want to opt out of that pissing contest? Don't fancy climbing a career ladder, when every time you get halfway up some cunt adds another ten rungs at the top? You'll find no quarrel from me.

For the rest of us? Well, if we dream of bigger things but it does our nut in having to work for someone else, we need to take matters into our own hands. Some people just aren't cut out for working for others, and I'm one of those people. Entrepreneurial spirit has been there the whole way through, for me, but that's just the natural demeanour of millions of hungry poor kids. Apart from my short time in the Indian restaurant and that desk job Michael sorted me out with, I never really had a normal job and I always felt like I lived on the edge. From being on the streets to what I'm doing now, my life's mainly been commission work of one sort of another, which is a double-edged sword. It means I can have a lie-in most mornings and work my own hours, but it also means my income can be precarious. There've been times when I've had no work for two or three months, then in the fourth month I've made five months' worth of money. That's the sort of unpredictability that would make no sense to someone who's been in a waged job their whole lives – to some people, not being able to budget for the rest of the year would send them crazy.

But there's no doubt that when you're skint, and you're desperate, sometimes that's when you have your best ideas. The best ideas I've had, and some of the most lucrative, have been when I've been flat out on my face. It opens your mind to think outside the box. If you're comfortable and everything's perfect for you, how can you think out of the box? You have no need to.

The hard part is not to take the easy option. There are definitely quick ways to make money, but they'll get you banged up. Having said that, if you've ever shotted and been on the road, you've probably picked up some decent transferable skills. I mean, it's basically just customer services. In my teens I dealt with probably every type of person, from down-and-out crackheads to estate agents in cheap suits and the sons and daughters of aristocrats, and through doing that I ended up becoming a pretty good judge of character. If you want to teach a robot artificial intelligence, put them out on the road in south-west London for a month; body language, eye contact, speech, the meaning behind words … you pick up on the lot. I probably owe my life to the times someone was chatting happily to me, but I picked up something about their body language that told me they were going to try to kill me.

Anyway, my point is, if you've had enough experience of that life, you can use your talents somewhere else. And probably somewhere you're not going to get shot. And trust me, if you've sold drugs once in your life, you can sell anything. All the principles are the same: whether it's milk, tea or condoms you're selling something everyone wants. And, if you've bought them in at a good enough price, you can make money on those deals.

Think of your average café. Not your 'artisanal sour-dough' place where you get your brunch served on an old roof tile. A proper café, which doesn't even have an 'é' in its name: it's a caff, with old-school, mug-of-tea-on-the-side, coronary-on-a-plate breakfasts. They'll buy a can of pop 50p wholesale, sell it for a quid, and double their money. And chips! How much are potatoes? They're literally as cheap as chips. A portion of chips you'll sell for a quid is only about 7p worth of potato. Everyone's a dealer. Everyone's hustling. You can too.

And yeah, it's easier to hustle if you've been around hustlers your whole life – you've inherited the hustling mindset. But you can pick it up anytime, just from being around the right people. The ultimate example has to be *The Apprentice*: we've all watched enough of that to know these people are all fucking idiots, and yet they talk them-selves into jobs and money. The common denominator: seeing is believing.

Right now the ultimate hustle is over on Instagram, and I've got mad respect for anyone who can make something out of nothing like those people making a living out of being an influencer. They don't even need to buy a 7p potato; the right photo in front of the right wall, and they're set. But there's also bare people launching their own products on socials and getting rich as a result. It's probably never been a better time to have an entrepreneurial spark – there's nothing to stop you putting this book down right now, designing a

T-shirt, promoting a few posts with a couple of quid and having orders flooding in by tomorrow evening.

So while it's true that there are all sorts of things that could get in the way of you having a decent career – setbacks, dead ends, tough times when you were growing up – it's also true that there are some open goals in your life, and you just need to take the shot. It's about looking forward and having the balls to try.

7

KNOWING YOUR ROOTS: COMMUNITY'S KEY

Part of functioning as a human is knowing yourself, and part of knowing yourself is understanding where you come from. I don't just mean your home address (though that's not something you can ever take for granted after a big night out); I mean truly grasping where you grew up.

For me, that means Brixton: not just its streets, houses and shops, but the people who brought it all alive. In the nineties, Brixton was vibrant, dangerous and exciting. Acre Lane, where I spent most of my time, felt like the heart of it all, but when I think of the Brixton I grew up in, I think of one word above any other, and that word is community.

They say it takes a village to raise a child and it was definitely true that a lot of children in my local community were raised not only by their parents – many parents were working long hours, or not around at all – but by the friends and family living on the same street. I remember it was these people (Mrs Davis, Mrs Washington, Sister Ivy, Mr Bigger) who helped man when he kicked his ball over their fence, or helped me with my pushbike. They told me not to do naughty things and even stopped me when my parents weren't around to step in.

And it wasn't just me who felt the positive force of that community. It was all the kids my age. There was a guy in our community who was good at fixing pushbikes, who taught kids how to fix their mountain bikes. Another who was good at kicking a football, and trained us up; another, an artist, who painted with us. These weren't people who were doing it for money – they just wanted to share their experience and knowledge with others. The community saved us when we got run over, and they were calling an ambulance when someone had been shot or stabbed; holding a teenager's belly together with a towel until the medics arrived.

It was so united. Most of the disputes in that community – and don't get me wrong, there were plenty of disputes – could be sorted out by and within the community. We knew ourselves, we understood ourselves, we knew how to settle quarrels before they got out of hand. The elders in our community might have told me off, but if I was being hassled by the cops and the police were wrongfully dealing with me, that same neighbour wouldn't think twice about coming out and going: 'What are you fucking doing? Let Tyrone go.'

And back then, this was before there was CCTV pointing round every street corner and down every alley. There was no all-seeing-eye like there is now. People say you should feel safer with cameras everywhere but as far as I'm concerned the only good thing about a camera is to see who killed you, and it's a bit fucking late by that point. If you know inner cities, you know that a camera doesn't determine whether or not some bloke's going to blow your head off with a gun. Real talk: a guy will pull you out of your car on the high road in broad daylight, he'll take your car, he'll get it to a chop shop and it'll be in a shipping container on its way to Nigeria the next day. He'll do all of that in front of the big all-seeing-eye, and he's not going to give a shit. Look around where you're living and know this: your mum isn't safe on the streets because of cameras; she's safe because of your community.

And it might sound mental given how much crime there was in the area, but in Brixton we never locked a door or a window. I know you're thinking, 'Come on, bruv, old people always go on about how in the olden days nobody locked their doors and that has to be bullshit', but it's true. We never experienced a random burglary. Somehow, the community looked after itself. There were nights I'd come in fucking out of my box, so off it that I'd leave my keys in the front door, and the door wide open, before stumbling in and ending up face down on the floor. The next morning I'd find that a neighbour had shut the door, taken the keys out and posted them through the letterbox. Look out for your neighbours, and they'll look out for you.

These days, though, that sort of behaviour isn't so common. London represents the whole of our country's multicultural diversity and Brixton, especially, will never

ever lose the Afro-Caribbean heritage that's been part of it for generations – that's implanted in it now. But nowadays the faces and backgrounds of Brixton inhabitants have changed, and the community just isn't so much of a community any more. These days, the neighbourhood would feel funny saying something to another person's kid, or defending them if the cops were shaking them down. When half the community's been replaced by people from different classes, different backgrounds and different cultures, the remaining half is looked after half as well.

When I grew up, there were only two worlds: the community in and around my street, just off Acre Lane, and then main Brixton. I spent most of my time round my block so I was in a community. Now, with people who've moved in over the last ten or fifteen years into newly built apartment blocks, expensively renovated houses with fucking glass boxes on the back of them and places like my old converted school, there are three worlds. Physically those worlds are all on top of each other, but in terms of community they might as well be in different cities. Civilians and normal 9-to-5ers would walk down the same roads as us day in day out, but for them the roads are used for different things. It's like we are invisible to each other.

As a result, the Brixton I see now is gentrified. Parts of it have changed beyond recognition from the shithole I remember from my youth. There's couture shops now, and coffee shops, and couture and coffee shops, and a modern 'event space' (i.e. another coffee shop) on Acre Lane. We've always been able to pick up second-hand clothes in Brixton, but now the charity shops are more likely to be 'vintage' outlets (same shit, twice the price).

The music venue Electric is a renovated version of the Brixton Fridge club I'd go to as a kid, and the road behind it used to be something I'd use every day as a cut-through to get up towards Brixton Hill and over to Olive Morris House. Nowadays that cut-through isn't there any more: they've built posh houses there, and the road's blocked off. There's no more cut-through. That sums up the bad side of gentrification for me: I'm fine with things changing, but existing communities are now faced with something they can't use. Memory Lane has turned into a dead end.

There are aspects of Brixton's newly affluent status that I don't mind, though. I mean, if you're going to give people an opportunity, and if you agree that giving people an opportunity is good, you can't really be upset with them if what they do with that opportunity (like move to Brixton) doesn't suit your own world view. And there are people I grew up with in my community who invested in Brixton in the early seventies and are reaping the benefits now – people who were able to save and make sacrifices and get on the housing ladder back then, who've now found themselves in houses worth a million quid.

If you had the money back then but weren't smart enough to buy your house in 1976 when it was worth £150, you're a fucking prick. Obviously, though, not everyone on my block was lucky enough to have enough spare pennies lying around for their electric meter, let alone enough to consider ever buying a house. It's those people who've been hit hardest by gentrification: they haven't benefitted at all from the rise in house prices, and have in fact found themselves squeezed out of the area altogether. They've seen all the downsides and none of the benefits, and they've seen their community – the one thing you could rely on even when times were tough – slowly fall apart.

And I don't want you to think I'm pulling a total rose-tinted-glasses trick on you here. There were sides of the community that weren't so positive. But the exceptions were truly exceptional. Thinking back, the barbershop on Tintern Street, where I've been having my hair cut since I was six years old, was a real social hub. The typical vibe of the place is that there's blokes shouting the entire time and halfway through cutting they'll stop, put their kit down and have a passionate 45-minute chat about the cricket. It's no place for a quick trim, but, in a way, the barbershop was the first male mentorship I really experienced: loads of men in one room talking, and talking freely. For a lot of the older guys there, who'd hang out regardless of whether they needed a haircut or even whether they actually had any hair, it was probably the closest they ever got to therapy. As a young kid I didn't always know what they were talking about but the laughing, joking and arguing was all about camaraderie. They were always cussing each other, but at the same time a lot of things were talked out and aired in that barbershop. Big topics. If something was going on in the news, or even just in the local community, it was going to be discussed in the barbershop. (If you're feeling a bit out of sorts, your own local barbershop might be a good place to get stuff off your chest.)

Beyond all that, one of the most inspirational people (and the most righteous role model) I've ever met was at my local church. Pastor Chris was like man's dad. In fact, he was a lot of kids' dads. Our church youth centre regularly had 40 kids in it, and if you're wondering how important that sort of social hub really is, get this: when the church centre got closed down, within a year five of those kids were dead and eighteen were in jail. I didn't realise it when I was making music or drawing with Pastor Chris, but every Monday and Wednesday those six hours I spent at the youth centre were six hours I wasn't on the road. Six hours without older men giving you drugs to go and sit on the block with.

Pastor Chris was the guy who scraped together the money to take a group of us to Chessington World of Adventures; some weekends he'd take 20 of us from the block on bicycle rides. He'd take us over to Forest Hill, to the Horniman Museum where we'd laugh at the stupid stuffed walrus. Pretty modest days out, all told, but we'd never have done any of these things without Pastor Chris.

Because, to us, our whole world was Brixton. Put it this way: we thought Croydon, just a few miles down the road, was a different country. Those famous Ikea chimneys that stick out on the horizon as you look down Purley Way might as well literally have been in Sweden. Back then our minds were so small and so stuck in one place, and our lives were so entwined in the back streets, that we felt the rest of the world, even a few streets away, wasn't ours. We didn't understand life beyond Brixton, but we'd been brought up to understand that it didn't want us.

Except Pastor Chris didn't think small. His mind was so open. He once told me: 'You can *be* stuff. The world is bigger than Brixton.'

Until he said that I think I would have been satisfied to stay in Brixton forever. But as soon as he said it, and showed us the world beyond SW9, it was hard for my mind to stay there. I always think that when you're a kid you can't miss what you don't know, but think of it like this: once you've had a Five Guys burger, how does a McDonald's taste? When you've had Copella cloudy apple juice, you don't want Asda concentrate any more. It feels like you've experienced the truth. You've opened your eyes. And once you've tasted the truth, it's hard to go back.

Obviously, that creates a tension: you want to move forward, but life doesn't seem to want to let you get out of the box you're in. For me, I couldn't figure out how to get out of the situation I was in around Brixton. It was like being in an escape room: you know there has to be a way out, because you know other people have got out before you, but all you can see before you is a series of impossible tasks. I couldn't see the route out; all I could see was what was pulling me down a certain path that (inevitably, it seemed) led to drugs, violence and prison.

Particularly given the fact that my brother had gone down that path, and was in prison by the time I was in my teens, my mum was really strong on my getting out of Brixton. She'd say: 'Just fucking get out.' It's hard to hear that kind of thing from your own mother. When she was telling me to get out of the community I'd always thought of as home, I thought she hated me and that she didn't want me around. The realest thing she said to me during that period was when she went: 'Son, you know that thing you're sitting here in Brixton waiting for? It's not going to happen for you in Brixton. Stay here and you'll still be in the same place, in the same road, doing the same thing ten years from now. If you don't get out and try and see the world, and not just the world you know, you'll be stuck.'

I didn't understand it at the time: I thought she was just a fucking bitch who wanted me gone. But then I remembered those endless afternoons I'd spend sitting at my mum's kitchen table with ten boxes of cigarettes piled up and nothing going on in my life, and I thought: I can do this. I'm not a big book reader but one I do recommend is Rhonda Byrne's book *The Secret*, a book about positive thinking that had a massive impact on me at the time. But no impact was greater than those words my mum had said to me. I thought: 'I'm going to get out of this shithole.'

I had no resources at that point, just the power of positive thought and the fact that my music career was starting to take off, although by that point it still wasn't making any money. But it all came into play. I started to ignore the fact that I was supposedly destined to stay in Brixton forever. I'm like the new dictionary definition of the bumblebee. Now, bumblebees aren't supposed to fly. Think about the ratio of body weight to wing size. Fucking ridiculous creatures, really, and scientifically they shouldn't be able to get off the ground. Thing is, though, a bumblebee doesn't know that. The bumblebee isn't reading books about bumblebees. He sees himself as a normal bee, and he knows he needs to get to the flower to pollinate. So he just takes off. He might take a strange route and bounce off a few things on the way, but the bumblebee still pollinates. In life, the bumblebee is worth remembering: sometimes you just need to follow your own path, not worrying about whether or not you 'should' be able to do something.

In urging me to leave Brixton – and pulling a few strings behind the scenes with my label Dice Recordings – my mum saved my life. I'm 100% certain that if I'd just stayed in Brixton I'd never have become the man I am now. I'd have a hole in my head the size of a 50p piece, or I'd be in a dustbin somewhere, or I'd be doing 45 years. If I hadn't moved in 2004, I feel like I could have ended up killing someone by now. The fact that my mum pushed me away ended up being the right thing. Looking back, it probably broke her heart that she had to push me forwards like that, but she made me have a life, and I don't think I'd have had one worth living if I'd stayed in Brixton. There was just no *space* for me there.

And so, I ended up in Essex. A place with its own personality, but just close enough to the north of north London to still feel connected. Now Essex's not exactly the middle of nowhere but I'll tell you, after a couple of decades in SW9 it feels like wide open countryside in comparison. I came to Essex and I saw paddling pools and pub gardens. I thought: 'It's not me, but I appreciate it.' I realised I could do silly little things, like just sitting in the park, without hearing police sirens. I'd see mums and dads with their kids, rather than just the kids, and nobody was nicking their bikes. None of the dogs had muzzles on them, because they weren't the sort of dogs that needed muzzles. Just free-roaming dogs, who didn't want to bite your face off! I even saw families having fucking *picnics*.

I guess a lot of people think that's just normal stuff, but I'd never seen that normal stuff except on TV. Even though I was living in a shit flat with mould so bad it nearly killed me, within a few weeks of moving to Essex I felt, for the first time, like I had a future ahead of me. I even found myself daring to think about having a full-on family.

'One day,' I remember thinking, 'I'll be coming to the park with my kids and the dog and having a stroll.' (A stroll! A walk for no reason! Nobody goes for a stroll in Brixton.) It was nice, truth be told. Weird, but nice. And after years of everybody knowing my name, my background and my business, I could go and walk in a field and I was *no one*. I mean, I was someone, but I was still, brilliantly, absolutely no one. I get recognised less now I'm on TV and living in Essex than I did the whole time when I was 15 and living in Brixton.

One thing that took a lot of readjustment was the sudden realisation that I was basically the only black person in the village. Well, not quite – there was a black guy called Alvin who lived a couple of streets away – but before moving to Essex I'd never experienced being in a minority. Brixton was black. It was Harlem. To give you an idea of what Brixton was like, there were maybe seven white people in my entire year at primary school. If I wanted to be surrounded by white people I'd have to go to Bromley or New Addington or Croydon. My friends from north London and east London would often tell me stories about growing up with white boys in their area. My bredrin' Nathan, who's from north London, grew up in a white community and he had to put up with the National Front in his area – we never had that sort of thing where I lived and I don't think things would have ended well for a group of Nazis if they'd ever tried any of their bullshit on Acre Lane. (Strange isn't it that they never came looking for trouble in Brixton, almost as if they're a bunch of pussies.)

So mingling with what I'd grown up seeing as 'proper English culture' was exciting, and weird: it was like being a Japanese tourist in Central London. I was out of my comfort zone – but I still felt comfortable. Moving out of my Brixton bubble has helped me see life in a different way, and to see a future for myself in a way I hadn't dared see one before. I can also see a brighter future for my family, with more opportunities for my kids. There are schools here where they even play rugby. Rugby! There's no school in Brixton playing rugby. None of them have even got playing fields.

Maybe you've got your own 'Brixton' – the place where your roots are – and your own 'Essex': that place where you can put down some roots of your own. Maybe you're happy where you are, or maybe you just think you are. Either way, you need to know that you're never just stuck in one place. And thinking beyond the boundaries others have set for you, or that you've set yourself, can open up whole new worlds.

I'm happy with everything Brixton's made me to be, but I'm happy that Brixton and the community around me also made me the sort of person who could eventually feel able to leave it behind, and in doing that I've had other experiences and knowledge of how life works outside Acre Lane.

I needed to leave Brixton to live my life, but it's also true that the biggest part of me will always be Brixton.

And anyway, it's not as if I'm never there. While I sleep and raise my family in Essex, it's rare that more than a few days passes when I'm not in Brixton for one reason or another. My mum and her family, along with most of my mates, are still in the area.

And if I have invitations to go to a block party in Brixton or some fancy place in town, I'll still choose the block party every time.

And I'll always bring the rice and peas.

8

TECH: USE IT, BUT DON'T LET IT USE YOU

Right now the big thing in tech is artificial intelligence. AI is all about robots trained by humans to be more human than human and eventually kill us all. Well, fair enough, strictly speaking that's not the plan, and right now computers are just doing what they're told, but I think we all know how it plays out.

You might be wondering: 'Should I embrace technology with both hands? Or should I throw my phone in the bin and go and live off-grid in a shed made from scavenged planks?' My real advice would probably lie somewhere in the middle. Part of me quite likes the idea of living like Sarah Connor with a bunker full of explosives and guns but the more we kill off real human emotion, and the more we leave things to synthesised versions of ourselves, the closer we are to the world being blown up by some metal fucker with a death wish. And anyway, I don't know if 'making computers as intelligent as humans' is really the right way of thinking about it. Don't know about you, but I've met some pretty fucking stupid humans in my time.

And look, I know Mr Amazon didn't really have the termination of human existence on his mind when he decided to start flogging Echo machines, any more than Tim Berners-Lee was thinking of arseholes doing God-knows-what on the dark web when he invented the internet, but what a lot of these people forget when they're making things to make our lives better is that they're just as readily available to people who want to make our lives worse.

Real talk, when someone can just email you an attachment and the next thing you know you're 3D printing a fully working gun, you know we're in trouble. People are rushing to make great inventions without really understanding the true costs. It reminds me of that line in *Jurassic Park*: 'ARGGHHH!' But also: 'Your scientists were so preoccupied with whether or not they *could*, they didn't stop to think if they *should*.'

A short story about how tech can absolutely fuck us all. A few years back I got a text message off a mate who was behind bars. Obviously you're not supposed to have a smartphone when you're banged up, but the thing you need to remember about people in prison is this: THEY'RE ALL FUCKING CRIMINALS AND SOMETIMES THEY BREAK RULES. Anyway, where there's a will (and by will I mean large enough anal cavity) there's a way, and there he was in his bunk messaging me. He was missing his family, he said. He was homesick. And then it came: 'Bro, let me use your Facebook login, just so I can see pictures of my family.'

He was bored off his nut and I didn't see any harm in letting him use my account to connect with his family, so I sent back the login details. He wasn't a big social media user, but then neither am I, and I barely used my Facebook back then, so I didn't think any more of it.

Several months later, me and the missus are out for dinner together: nothing posh, just a midweek date in Nando's and a bit of relaxing time away from our mad lives. And during the gap between ordering our food and our plates actually arriving I noticed this bird from across the room making mad eye contact with me. Even after the food arrived she was still at it, looking more and more angry as the evening went on. By the time we were onto our brownies she'd gone into total if-looks-could-kill mode: the evilest looks you've ever seen, straight down into my soul.

Eventually, when I get up for a refill, she comes over to me and fully lets me have it: 'You're texting me all night saying you want to get to know me, while you're in here with another girl?' I just have no idea what's happening, but she goes on, and on. 'YOU DON'T KNOW WHO I AM?'

By this point my missus was getting involved. And if you've ever been to Nando's you won't be surprised to hear that the unfolding drama was picking up the attention of the rest of the restaurant, too. One geezer even repositioned his chair so he could get a better view of the free cabaret show. Eventually this woman gets her phone out, fires up Facebook and waves it in my face. You've probably filled in the gaps by now: my mate hadn't been 'catching up on family pictures' at all – for months, he'd been using my Facebook account with my fucking name and photo on it, trying to chat up women. And he'd been sexting this one particular girl for *weeks* using my Facebook account.

I said to this girl: 'You've been talking to my mate.' She wasn't having a bar of it – she cussed me out in front of everyone and stormed out, leaving me to deal with my missus.

And that, in a nutshell, is why I've got a problem with our over-reliance on technology. It's not personal, you've got no idea what anyone's really fucking doing or even who they are, and if it falls into the wrong hands you're in a whole heap of trouble. The lesson here: don't believe everything you see in your phone. Also, don't give your mates your logins.

I'm not saying all technology's shit; it's just that, being the age I am, I remember the days before we were all walking around with the internet in our pockets – when not every house even had internet in it, and those that did were still on dial-up.

My first mobile phone came along when I was about twelve. I can still remember the model: it was a Sony Eriksson T28 that had a flip-down speaker bit, a black and white screen that had enough space for about one line of text, and a massive aerial sticking out the top. I bought it off a crackhead who, it turned out, was very much in demand.

For the first couple of weeks I kept answering the phone to geezers yelling, 'I'M GOING TO KILL YOU', so it wasn't long before I had to get my own SIM card. Back then when me and the mandem didn't have enough credit we'd get around it by sending voicemails backwards and forwards like a really shit walkie-talkie setup, but the one bit of tech I really miss from that era is the pager.

I won't go into detail about what exactly I was using my pager for but I do know that if I tried to explain the idea of pagers to kids now they'd think I was mad. Back then, and this was before many people had mobile phones, if you wanted to get in touch with someone who had a pager you'd call a special number, which would be answered by a human being, then you'd tell them your short message and then they'd type it into a computer and beam it to this pebble-size thing with a screen that your mate was carrying. Oh, and they couldn't reply: if your mate wanted to get back to you, they'd have to find a fucking payphone. My pager back then was more of a fashion statement, to be honest, but it could be helpful for work...

Truth be told, most of the time when I was coming up I didn't really need a phone. My mum's house was like a headquarters for our family and, where we lived, three of my best friends lived on the same road and the other two were on the next road along, which meant our back gardens were facing each other. Everything was in reach, and everyone was close by – we could climb from my back garden to the high road, all through back gardens. It was an agility test, but I was quite a daredevil back then. I used to like jumping from high things, and I was really into kung fu films, so you'd often find me trying to do a front flip out of a first-floor window. My ultimate objective back then was to be a ninja: I never mastered the backflip but I definitely tried on numerous occasions. (I could probably still do a handstand now, you know. In fact, I did a hand-spring into a swimming pool just the other day.) Point is: I didn't need a phone to be in touch with my mates. Try to separate a kid from their phone now and you'll come away with a broken arm.

One thing I'm certain of with technology is that whether it's through climate crisis or some future version of an already-existing robot, mankind has already invented whatever it is that will bring about mankind's own demise. And maybe that's fine. Maybe we've had our chance: we were given a planet; it was inevitable we'd fuck ourselves and now here we are.

All I'm saying is, don't come running to me one day when some robot walks into a room, shouts, 'ALEXA: DESTROY THE WORLD', and within 90 minutes a global network of millions of online devices has totally wiped out the lot of us. I mean, you won't come running to me anyway because you'll have had your face fried off by a malfunctioning internet-connected microwave, but you won't be able to say I didn't warn you.

So I don't have an Alexa at home – I don't want something listening to me in my house. Fuck the police! That entire listening smartspeaker thing is *totally* fuck the police. The whole point of paying to live somewhere is that you have privacy, so then why would you pay again to have a little white tube in the corner listening to everything you say? No, thanks. If you're inviting one of those into your home, you might as well sleep naked on the local park bench and shout all your secrets at random passers-by while your cock and balls sway back and forwards in the evening breeze.

My one totally unquestioning concession to enjoying technology is gaming, which is mainly what I do in my downtime. People might think I'm always mingling in the upper echelons of the entertainment business, hobnobbing in fancy bars, but chances are if I'm not working, and once the kids are in bed, I'll be in my boxer shorts playing *Call of Duty*, saving the world in my underpants, or I'll be on the toilet with my phone playing *Rise of Kingdoms*, sending my scouts out to find gold and forage for food, looking for wood while I'm laying some logs of my own.

Gaming's been a passion from when I was a kid. Xbox, Amiga, Commodore, Sega Megadrive – these are the consoles and computers I've loved, lost, and come back to, and they'll always have a special place in my heart. Even the titles of the games bring the past flooding back: *Alex Kidd, Altered Beast, Mortal Kombat, Sonic the Hedgehog, Zelda.*

MOTHERFUCKING *ZELDA.* When you see the older 16-bit graphics now, it's amazing to think this is what was keeping us up and entertained for hours, but every time I get on the controls of an old game it's like I get to relive the better parts of my childhood – it's like I'm suddenly being connected with the younger version of myself. How mad is it that something that once seemed like it was from the future ends up being more like a portal back to the past?

So you can imagine how chuffed I was in 2016 when I got to launch my own game for smartphones. It was called *Base Invader*s and you control a little cartoon version of the ultimate base invader (i.e. me), firing massive spliffs at policemen. Within a week on the app stores it was topping music and arcade app charts and hit the overall UK charts in the Top 5. I mean, it didn't exactly shift *Fortnite* numbers, but it did pretty well for my first game.

One of the good things about the explosion in tech over the last 10 or 15 years is how much it's made possible for kids who don't have much money or resources back home. So much of what I'm doing now is down to the Uncle Pain videos I started doing a few years back where people would contact me with their problems and I'd solve them in my own way: the realest motherfucking agony uncle you could ever meet.

I started them nine years ago and, like many of the best things, it happened totally by accident when me and my mate Lordie were in the car. I said: 'Imagine if man did like a Jerry Springer show.' He seemed to like that idea. We made up five questions in the car and just went for it, uploading video after video of Uncle Pain dishing out advice, and before long we didn't need to make up problems because we were getting thousands of emails with real problems.

With that, came millions of YouTube views. Uncle Pain was fun while it lasted. I found that people really appreciated a real unmediated opinion and not a playsafe, politically correct one: things were straight between me and the people watching it. Right up to the end, the emails to Uncle Pain kept on coming. What I liked about being able to interact with people was that it felt like a special two-way relationship that had an instant feel I wouldn't really have been able to have with Uncle Pain's viewers before social media. I didn't think of it too much at the time – it was just talking real shit in the car smoking weed, and none of it was done like we were trying to 'do something' because it was just man having fun – but it was one of those rare times when I've been online and the backwards and forwards felt both genuine and authentic.

Considering I'm a bit of a caveman in some respects it's pretty fucked up that I've become so big on social media, and it's even more surprising to me that I enjoy myself so much, chatting on Twitter, throwing up candids on Instagram and all the rest.

I've got someone on my team who can be 'me' on socials, and that's Shar. She helps with posting at the right time for some of the business-related posts, but the rest are 100% me. It's not like I have a whole company to do everything for me, like some famous people have. That's just madness and doesn't sit right for me at all. If you're following me it's important to me that you know you're getting the real deal on Twitter and Instagram, just the same as you get the real deal in my music. As far as I'm concerned, getting someone to write your tweets is every bit as fucked up and dishonest as getting someone else to write your bars. And yeah, it's true that plenty of other people do both those things, but it's not for me.

I try not to be too bothered about how many likes and retweets I get on posts because one of the biggest curses of social media is the obsession with knowing everybody else's opinion of you. You can drive yourself mad trying to get big numbers, and I know the big irony of the social world is that I could spend days of my life and thousands of pounds trying to pull together a piece of video content that would go viral, and in the end I'd probably get better numbers just posting a five-second vid I'd made on my toilet.

Approaching apps with caution is particularly true when it comes to dating online and through apps. The thing with technology is that it's given us a lot of information, but it's dulled a lot of people's social skills. Me, I'm from the era of walking down the high street, seeing a sexy girl, and saying: 'Excuse me, you look gorgeous, can I buy you a drink or get to know you?' If it's a no, it's a no, fair enough;

if it's a yes, it's happy days. But the point is that whatever the answer, I always felt that I'd at least been judged on who I really was, standing in front of her. Now everything is swiping left and swiping right and it means people aren't talking to real people.

One thing I will say is that it's all very well for me, not exactly a shy and retiring wallflower, to say it's sad that communication has changed, but I suppose for anyone who grew up shy it's a lot easier for them to be able to meet others online than, say, bouncing up to someone in the street. Not all people are comfortable and can talk to people and chat them up.

But however confident or however self-conscious you are, you need to know that what you're seeing online isn't real. Think of all those people who post their delicious-looking, perfectly presented plates of food on Insta when it's time for dinner: you don't also see the fucking sink stuffed with dirty pans, do you? You don't see the overflowing kitchen bin or the mouse droppings in the corner. If you want to get the full picture of what someone's like, you need to see it with your own eyes – and not through a screen.

The fact that people can exist solely on one side of the black mirror brings me to another big problem with the online world: trolls. Or as I like to think of them: cunts. I'm not being funny but if we did away with the word 'troll', and just called these people cunts, we'd save ourselves a lot of pain.

I used to wonder what sort of people trolls were. What was it that was driving them to spout all this bile and bull-shit at other people online? And then I realised that nine times out of ten it's just people with too much time on their hands. There's one true thing here: when you're busy you don't see things, and when you're not busy you do. And by that I mean, there's no way you can do an 18-hour shift at work, then play with your kids, then spend time with your partner and then still have time to go on Twitter and say horrible things to people. What's their real life looking like? Pretty empty – we're not generally dealing with people who've got a lot going for them. More specifically, what's their *room* looking like? I don't think I want to know, but I can tell you there's a pretty disgusting pile of used Kleenex next to their laptop.

So like a lot of bullying I reckon trolling is more of a cry for help, or a cry for attention. How we deal with it is the question. Now I'm not a big fan of horror films – in fact I hate them, and if one comes on the TV I just turn the TV off – so my general advice with trolls is to do the same: ignore these people and shut the app. Or even better, mute them or block them, and carry on using the app exactly as much as you like, as if that little annoyance on the bottom of your shoe had never existed.

Having said that, it's hard to not to take the bait, and I still sometimes fall for it – but it's interesting how revealing an exchange can sometimes be. Not so long ago some guy on Twitter took time out of his busy (i.e. not busy) day to tweet me: 'You fat dickhead'.

I mean I can call myself fat, and I can call myself a dickhead, and my mates can call me both, but I got the impression this keyboard warrior wasn't exactly tweeting me from a position of friendliness. I had two options: go in all guns blazing and turn this all into the mother of all Twitter beefs, or try to shut it down. I went for the killing-with-kindess route, and wrote back: 'I love you too, my bro. We'll burn a spliff if I see you.'

Within five minutes he'd tweeted me back: 'I'm so sorry, you're such a real G, I just didn't know what to say.'

Just like that, this situation that could have got ugly just fizzled into nothing. I'd been dealing with someone who was just like one of those boys who pulls girls' hair in the play-ground, desperately hoping for some attention but unable to articulate himself in a mature way. But do you know what? If that bloke does bump into me one day, maybe we will still burn a spliff together. Maybe he's a decent guy – but I'd want to look him in the eye first to find out.

But this is the thing with the online world. The planet is full of people who need to be heard and the internet means they can be, but it's also full of people who just *want* to be heard, and some of these people are the last people on earth who should get any attention at all. They're stuck using McDonalds' free wifi, they're angry about the world, and they're taking it out on other people.

And that's the one thing my generation, or anyone who rejects the idea of totally buying into the facelessness of technology, will always have over and above anyone who lives their life online. They might have more information, but they've lost all their feeling. There's no point in having data if you don't know what to do with it, or if you don't know what any of it really *means*. Don't mistake having the world's information at your fingertips for having the intelligence to know what to do with it.

Compassion, love, education, understanding, legacy, tradition: these are all things worth being kept alive, and you won't find those in the settings of your Samsung. Real life is one thing; your phone life is another thing. You should never allow yourself to believe they're the same.

9

LAW AND DISORDER: AVOID THE SPIRAL

If you talk to a person in prison, their world view is that everything is limited: 'I don't know if I could do that', 'fuck doing this', 'fuck doing that'. Unless they're nonces or rapists, I don't understand why more inmates aren't just sent to work in the army and make something of their lives, truth be told, but my point is that it's easy in prison, or in life in general, to find yourself surrounded by negativity, to the point where you can't see any glimmer of positivity at all.

If you grow up around a lot of crime, you can find it's that sort of negativity that dominates your field of view.

Until my early teens my main male role models came from pop culture: wrestlers, Buju Banton, anyone who'd been in a ninja film, and Shabba Ranks. But in my local community around Acre Lane it felt like the only role models I saw happened to be drug dealers. It wasn't their work that seemed appealing, but their lifestyles – with only a couple of exceptions (like Tony, who ran the barbershop, and Cliff, the first man I knew to have a phone in his BMW), it seemed to me that every single black person

I saw who was in a financially good place had achieved it through drugs, or through robbery, or through both.

When you've got mums bringing up kids alone – through no fault of their own – boys are going to find their own male role models, and when kids come out of their front doors and go to a local shop and all they're seeing is negativity, and violence, the only success that kid'll see in a poverty stricken area is via drug dealers. And success, in that sort of environment, doesn't mean much. It can be as trivial as seeing that a drug dealer won't have to wait until the end of the month before he can buy chicken and chips. You might have to wait, but the drug dealer can go to Chicken World right now and get whatever he wants.

I can't tell you not to covet lifestyles like that – they seem impressive, and aspiring towards them is, I guess, part of human nature. But I can tell you that people who lead those lifestyles haven't got to where they are without enduring a world of pain and shit, and causing hurt and suffering for others. Even when they're ordering their spicy chicken fillet mountain burger meal, they're still in pain. And I can tell you that because I've been there myself.

Every criminal starts somewhere, with a stupid minor transgression, and mine was about as stupid as they get. I remember it clearly: a March day in the early nineties, when I was still at primary school and Easter was on its way. Me and two mates snuck out during the morning, hurried over the zebra crossing outside the school, went into Tesco and each pocketed an Easter egg. Just a small one each – one of those Smarties eggs that must have been 99p since the dawn of time – so they were easy to hide in our big coats. Then we snuck back into school. Out and in and out and back in, job done.

And here's how the crime spiral works. After lunch (main course Easter egg, Smarties from inside the egg for dessert), I decided I wanted another Easter egg. Sick man that I am, I wanted to go back and get a massive, fat Rolo egg. I'd got away with it once, and this time I was going bigger. So in the afternoon after school it was back over the road and back into Tesco, and obviously as a kid I wasn't thinking about the practicalities – simple things like, 'where am I going to hide this massive Easter egg once I've nicked it?' I didn't consider that maybe security had seen me in there during the morning, and would keep an eye out for me if I went back, or that if you're running a Tesco opposite a school in Brixton, too right you're going to step up security after kicking out time. Long story short, I was strolling out with a gargantuan Rolo egg sticking out of my coat when I was grabbed by the security guard.

Next thing I know my mum's in the Tesco, shouting the place down. It might sound like I got off lightly but I'd probably have preferred it if they'd called the police. My mum is four foot six and I could fit her in my sidebag, but it's the little ones you've got to watch out for: when she gets mad she's like five Arnold Schwarzeneggers on steroids with suicide bombs on their chests, with George W. Bush's attitude. Trust me, when she gets on one, there's NO negotiating with terrorists.

We got home and – boom – she's put me down in the kitchen chair, and she's got this big kitchen knife.

She was just chatting away to me while the kitchen knife was heating up over the gas hob for ten minutes: 'You want to be a thief, yeah? See, in Jamaica, when you find people are thieves … I'll show you what they do with thieves in Jamaica …' By this point the knife was glowing red. She goes: 'Put your hand on the table.' I started crying! I mean, I'm laughing writing this, but at the time I was shitting it. She was going: 'Don't cry! Thieves don't cry!' Then she reached for the knife and held it above my hand … And I fainted! Straight on the floor, out for the count.

Obviously she was never going to follow through, but I now know exactly what she was doing: trying to scare the absolute living shit out of me. Trying to instil the fear. She'd seen other kids from my manor growing up, and where they were ending up in their teens: dead on the street, banged up behind bars. Thinking back about that day in the kitchen with the knife, and me ending up passed out on the floor, I know I was scared that day, but now I'm a parent myself I realise that however scared I might have been feeling, that's nothing compared to how scared my mum was feeling.

Particularly because of what she'd seen with my older brother. He was a prolific criminal from his early teens.

I remember seeing him pull the back off the TV (this was in the days before flatscreens) and there were straps, mobile phones, banknotes... All sorts were shoved in there. I'll never forget the evening we were all settling down to watch *Crimewatch* – every black person used to watch that show, and it was our big Sunday night programme. Me and him were playing Skalextric on the floor in the front room with *Crimewatch* on in the background. Mum's there in her chair too. And all of a sudden my big bro's on the fucking telly, wanted for robbery!

Within seconds the house phone had exploded with people going: 'I've just seen your brother on *Crimewatch*!' That was the end of our time on the Skalextric – he went on the run after that although he'd still pick me up after school, each time on a different, newly acquired mountain bike. He'd buy me Golden Wonder cheese and onion crisps, a Twix, and a Ribena. I saw everything from my brother.

It was strange for me seeing him doing all this stuff (and he was doing a lot of stuff), and getting away with it. My mum's take on the situation was slightly different. She told me: 'I am going to do everything in my power to make sure you don't go down the same road as your brother.'

But despite my mum's best efforts, it was out of her hands. If I had to pinpoint the time when I flipped, I'd say it was a night when I was nine years old. My bro was on the run again – people said he'd stolen loads of drugs, or money. Or maybe drugs and money. Maybe it was neither, but he was on the run anyway. One night all these guys came to my house – bashing in the front door, shouting. My mum rushed me to a cupboard, pushed me inside it and threw bare coats on me. She told me to stay there, and she shut the door on me.

In the darkness of that cupboard, covered in coats, I could hear those guys mashing up the front door. I could hear my mum shouting back at them: 'How can you give a fourteen-year-old fifty grand's worth of drugs? I ain't got fifty grand!' I heard them burst in turning the place upside down. They didn't find what they were looking for but they took all the Sky boxes and the TV. Then the noise stopped. I came out of the cupboard and saw my mum sitting on the stairs, crying.

I said to her: 'Don't worry, Mum. I'll be big soon.'

From there, I just went mad. I transgressed. I knew that the next time something like that happened, I wanted to be able to protect my mum, not be hiding in the cupboard like a little kid. I wanted to step up, and that's what I did. I was fuelled by anger and confusion.

The robbing came first. And it wasn't Rolo eggs this time – it was mobile phones and pushbikes.

I'd go to the park, ask if I could have a go on someone's bike, then I'd just ride the bike to Brixton Cash Converters. Bikes were the HUSTLE, cuz – get yourself a double suspension mountain bike and you're in the game for a straight £150. Sometimes it'd be me alone, sometimes it'd be me and mates. All these people had just gone to find some greenery and relax, then I'd appear on my bredrin's handlebars causing havoc. I was living the life of a barbarian. (My advice here is firstly not to go round robbing bikes in the first place, 'cos, legality aside, Cash Converters have stepped up their game since then and you'll have trouble shifting them. Secondly, if you're out on your bike and some little shithead asks for a go, politely decline.)

For phones, Pimlico was the spot. Me and the mandem would basically go to Pimlico on our lunch breaks and just terrorise the posh kids. Waiting until they'd left their phone out on a table, then grabbing it. One day they'd had enough of all this, and all the Asian kids started chasing us down the street. Every fucking man was there – I was running trying to get over Vauxhall Bridge and all I could hear was, 'GET THE FAT ONE! GET THE FAT ONE!' I knew if I looked back I was finished, and I had to keep my eye on the prize and RUN. I jumped on a bus in the end and as I whizzed away I saw that there'd been a man a few seconds behind me with a massive stick. My school shirt was transparent with sweat – I didn't even know I could run like that. The ones who got caught that day ended up in hospital, which I suppose served us all right.

Safe to say, I was getting into major trouble. Every other week I was doing something stupid. There was always an issue. In fact, one of the issues was that I kept getting hit by motorists. I was run over four times in that period, although I'm pleased to report that each time it was by a fancy car: a BMW, a Mercedes, a Jaguar, then a Saab 900. When I got hit by the Saab, I'd robbed a pushbike and I was rolling pretty fast before I realised I'd made the schoolboy error of nicking a bike without any brakes – I tried to put my foot on the back wheel to do a skid but because it was wet I couldn't get a grip, so I was going way too fast into Concanon Road and ended up in front of the Saab. Again, I suppose it served me right.

Looking back, the irony is that I'd first allowed myself to slip into this lifestyle because I'd wanted to be able to stand up for my mum and become a man, but I was actually making life far worse for her. She barely slept because she was so worried about what I was getting up to at night. She knew people were dying out there, and when she heard someone at the front door she'd never know if it was going to be me, someone looking for me, or the police with news about me. She'd hear about kids dying on the street, and she'd be thinking: 'Is it going to be my son today?'

In spite of that, my brother and I had a really open relationship with our mum, even if we were doing bad stuff. We could talk to her – and she made it clear that we didn't have to lie. When man's arrested, she'd come in and go: 'Yeah, but did you do it?' We'd have an open dialogue.

I mean, she'd still go fucking crazy, don't get me wrong. There were stages when I was fucking up, making mistakes, trying to find myself and I used to get SLAPPED. Every day! So my mum would always be having to come up with new ways of trying to instil some sense of right and wrong. Sometimes it'd be like: 'Right, so you want to get nicked and do stuff like that? Cool, you're going to clean all the skirting boards. You're going to wash clothes by hand in the bathtub, you're going to season meat all afternoon.'

Another time, she decided she'd try a three-strikes policy. You'd get your first warning, then your second warning, then after that the punishment was washing her back in the bath. Obviously as a kid, even a kid who's seen horror on the streets, nothing's quite as bad as having to wash your mum's back. She's naked in the fucking bath, and you're on your knees with soap on your hands washing her back. I washed her back *loads*. But my mum's a smart woman, and I only realise now how smart she was. I was washing her back so she was facing away from me and there was no eye contact when we talked. Even though I was there as a punishment I felt like I wasn't being judged. I got so much off my chest in those chats – I was so totally honest. I could say *everything*. That space to talk was really important. Whether you're a kid or a parent, you can't underestimate how important it is to have that sort of space in a relationship – if you find it, cherish it. And if you don't, try to create it.

When my brother was robbing banks and I was doing all sorts on the road, my mum wouldn't accept drug money and she refused to take robbery money. We all sometimes wonder what real price there is on our principles, but I can absolutely tell you that my mum's honour could not be bought with any money. She was going without meals so we could eat, working three jobs on minimum wage to keep a roof over our heads, and when me or my brother offered her money that we'd got through wrongdoings, she'd throw it back at us. My brother's robbing banks, bringing money home, and my mum's like: 'Get that out. Take that Devil money out of this fucking house.' At one point, she literally threw a bag containing £50K in banknotes out of the window onto the street, and I'll never forget what she told us afterwards: 'Even though I need the money, that's not the way I want to have it.'

My mum did all she could to sort me and my brother out, and she offered us unconditional love and a space to talk about our problems, but not accepting money from us was one of the biggest statements she could have made. There was no approval, no encouragement, no acceptance. It meant we couldn't tell ourselves that we were doing this for her. We couldn't kid ourselves we were behaving like savages 'for our mum'. In refusing to take our ill-gotten money she made us confront the fact that we were only doing this for ourselves. Neither me nor my brother can ever say that what we got up to was our mum's fault. We couldn't use her or anything else as a scapegoat for our wrongdoings.

This was on us, and it was up to us to get ourselves out of it. But that wasn't something I realised until later on.

Back in that moment, and despite my mum's best efforts, I was out of control by the age of 13, and by that point my brother was in prison.

My next step had been to start dealing drugs – or at least to pretend I was. One afternoon I was out on Acre Lane with my mate and this crackhead came up to us. 'Got anything?' he says.

'What?' I go.

And he says: 'You know what.'

And I'm stood there going: 'No, really mate, I don't know what.'

Eventually he just goes: 'CRACK!'

I didn't have any, obviously, but my mate goes: 'We can get it for you. How much do you want?'

The crackhead wanted forty quid's worth. We tried to get the money first and he told us to fuck off, which is fair enough. So we were like: 'Cool, meet you back here in an hour.' We went back to mine and tried to figure out what to do. Eventually I rummaged through my mum's kitchen cupboards and found some cornflour. At that point I had no idea what forty quid's worth of crack looked like so I dumped a load of cornflour in some clingfilm and we set out to meet our new best friend at the agreed rendezvous point. When the time came we showed him the 'drugs': a golfball-size boulder of cornflour. Like I say we didn't have a fucking clue what we were doing, and let's just say that amount of actual crack would have been worth a lot more than forty quid. The crackhead couldn't believe his luck: he grabbed the boulder, threw forty quid at us and ran off.

So that was that: my first drug deal, and it wasn't even drugs.

But after that, it wasn't cornflour. (Although sometimes it was – crackheads don't know what they're buying, and you can be out the door before they realise.) I started dealing a lot of weed, and through that I got to know the different types of addicts: a crackhead is erratic and fast-paced; a heroin addict is sick, and when they get sick there's no telling what they'll do. And there's nothing they *won't* do. A crackhead has a tiny bit more control than a heroin addict. A cocaine user, meanwhile, can be more civilised and more upper-echelon. (The horrible truth is that most of my time shotting drugs, it was so often to all the rich kids!) Weed users can vary.

Real talk though, the most extreme kind of addict I ever met during that period was the gambler. Trust me – plenty of addicts might be desperate, but you haven't met desperate until you've seen the look in the eye of a guy who seems totally normal but has just blown forty grand in a quarter of an hour. It still blows my mind that on every high street you'll get a line of properties that goes betting shop, payday loan shop, betting shop. The government won't legalise a drugs permit, but are happy to take taxes from these shops where you can go in and destroy your life whenever you fancy. I'm not in any position to advise you not to take drugs but I can tell you right now not to get involved in gambling. The house always wins, and your house ends up with no food in it.

I hadn't set out to be doing the things I was doing, but by 14 or 15 it had somehow become my life. Back in the day, everywhere I looked it seemed like there was only one message: you had to be a barbarian to make money. You had to get your hands dirty. There was a phrase I heard a lot back then from some of the elders on my block – 'desperation takes away cold feet'. That felt true to me. A desperate person will show you things you've never seen before. They'll astound you. The things they're doing aren't thought about: it's just pure animal instinct. Fight or flight, sink or swim, kill or be killed: these are all desperate situations.

Looking back, the scary thing is how normal it all seemed. It's like the kids you see on the news, living in Afghanistan, where the distant sound of bombs and guns is so everyday that when a bomb goes off, or a man's shot in the road, the kids don't even flinch. They've seen it a thousand times before and they'll see it a thousand times in the future. To them, it's just normal. And it was like that for me in Brixton. Growing up I saw violence, lawlessness and savagery on the street from the get-go. Nothing shocked me. Nothing scared me. It should have done.

As a kid the only way I'd ever thought I would get out of Brixton as a young black guy was through sport. Me and my mates saw Ian Wright and Linford Christie, and we knew that neither of those guys were making money because of their academic skills. They didn't go to college and university to get out, they made it out by doing sports. But I don't think I need to explain why a career as an athlete didn't seem like a viable option for me.

Instead, for a long period I thought my path was in the military, and the plan was that I'd become a bomb disposal specialist or a sniper in the army. If you're wondering why they appealed, I have one word for you: *Rambo*. I saw it and I thought: 'That's the job for me – saving people, shooting and fighting.'

The old kaboom squad might be high risk, but the adrenaline of knowing it could all go off at any moment appealed. The fact that I'd fallen behind at school was a problem because being a bomb disposalist you find that a lot of the job is about numbers and calculations: volume and space, blast radius, oxygen in the room dictating how far the bomb will blow, and so on. You don't just march in there with a hammer and a bucket and hope for the best. But despite my limitations, it felt like something to aim for. There was more chance of me doing that than becoming a footballer. My mum was encouraging and when I first told her I wanted to be in the army she wasn't shocked. She just told me: 'You'll have to work for it.'

So when I was old enough, it was suggested that I joined the army cadets, and I did get my corporal stripe but by that point I was so wayward that it was only going to end in disaster. There was this time we all went away for a week during the school holidays and I ended up spraining my leg on an obstacle course, which meant that I had to stay in the billets by myself the next day, while everyone else got to go to Alton Towers. So everyone else was off at Alton Towers, having the time of their life, and I'm just tidying up in the army billets. I thought: 'Fuck this, cuz.'

So I went for a wander. Just a *little* wander. I ended up in people's rooms, cleaning out the entire place. I came away with loads of chains, loads of money, loads of stuff. I totally cleaned up. I don't know what my plan was: I suppose I was thinking I'd end up selling it all, or giving it to girls I liked.

But then after everyone got back and realised they'd been robbed, I wore all their stuff to dinner. All their chains, all their jewellery. I was the only person who'd been there, so I'd have been a coward to hide the fact that it was me who'd done the robbing. You might think that surely I knew people would try to get their stuff back off me as soon as they saw me parading around the dinner table with it. But I just didn't care. That's where my mind was. Total self-sabotage scenes. As I'm older now, I wonder if it was all an elaborate cry for help or a really crap way of asking for people to just listen to me. But back then the message I was giving out was: 'I've taken everyone's fucking stuff, if you're men, just fight me for it.' I hadn't stuck it down my pants and pretended I didn't know what was going on. Did I feel there was some sort of honour in being honest about my robbing? It's like I was looking for some way I could establish my authority. I wanted to be able to be in control for once. I needed to say: 'I've taken your belongings; I'm a savage.'

What actually happened was that they all told the army police – I mean, of course they fucking did – and the army police arrested me. They kept me in a little room, talking shit at me: 'Aren't you worried for what you did?'

I was just thinking: 'You fucking idiots! You can't do shit – it's my mum who's going to smack my head in.' It all comes back to that glorious woman, that pint-sized dicta-tor. There's not a lot to my mum, but she has superpowers.

My grandma had once said to me: 'Sometimes you have to do bad to do good.' I think she told me those words in good faith. Let's say, for instance, your house is fore-closed – your kids are packed up in the back of the car, you haven't got a pot to piss in, and you see a box on the floor. It's got twenty grand in it. And of course, you should be a good samaritan and turn it in to the police. But – boom! What happens? You take that twenty grand, you pay the five grand you're owing on your mortgage, and you spend the other fifteen grand on setting up a business. Yes, you did fucking wrong, but you did it to get yourself in a good position. I think I took my grandma's words too much at face value. From that moment in the cupboard, covered in coats, when I decided I wanted to protect my mum, through the years afterwards when she made it clear she didn't even want the sort of protection I was able to offer, my mantra had shifted: instead of doing bad to do good, I was just doing bad, period.

My army career was over. After that, proper criminal records started happening. And all around me, mans were getting involved with guns. I saw a lot of shoot-outs. I don't know if you've ever been shot at it, but long story short I wouldn't recommend it. Point is, back then I just saw it as everyday life and I didn't care. When you're living your life like that and your day-to-day thoughts are basically 'this could be the last time I go to a shop, I might get shot on the way home', after a while it changes you for the worse.

I don't know where it might all have led had I not got in a fight with some guy and, as a result, been sent to a detention centre, which happened to be the 409 Project in Brixton, which is where I met Michael who in turn gave me that first desk job. Along with Pastor Chris at the church youth club, I credit Michael with not just changing my life but saving it. The 409 Project was the start of my rehabilitation: not something that happened overnight, and I made mistakes along the way, but I never would have made it out without that support.

There were dark times in my teens when I used to think about my situation and wonder what different stuff I could have done to make my situation better, and I figured that if I'd been given another option, I would have done anything to do things an alternative way. So when I found that I finally *did* have an opportunity to really see life, and make life, I grabbed that opportunity with both hands. I can't say this enough: there will be times in your life when it feels like nobody cares about you, and when you feel like there's nothing to stop you heading down the road to oblivion. But I believe most of us *do* have someone, somewhere, who wants to help. Never reject that help.

Having people I respected looking out for me and showing me a better way of living my life, 'I don't know any better' was no longer something I could claim – to myself or anyone else. Because from that point, thanks to Michael and Pastor Chris and the continued best efforts of my mum, I did know better. Perhaps it's easy to do fucked up shit if you really don't know any better, or if the only male role models in your life have gone down a certain path. But 'I don't know' didn't cut it any more because I *did* fucking know, and from Michael and Pastor Chris onwards I've been fortunate to have had loads of people pointing me in the direction of greatness.

You'd have to be a massive dick to keep going the wrong way when so many people have shown you the right way. Put it another way: if you accidentally drive off a cliff, that's not your fault. If the road you've been driving on has had warning signs every ten metres for three miles and you still end up upside down in a ditch, you can only blame yourself.

I was fortunate on my journey to meet educated people who tried to instil education in me, and open up my way of thinking. And I was fortunate that they persisted with me, even when I didn't want to listen. Along the way I found that I'd admired people for the wrong reasons, I'd admired status and status symbols, and I'd been too quick to use the phrase 'desperate times call for desperate measures' as an excuse for being a savage. I fell down and I picked myself up, again and again. I learned by trial and error. There was plenty of error. In fact, as my solicitor at the time would tell you, there were a few trials too. But I fucking learned.

10

MUSIC:
HOW A PASSION
BECOMES A CAREER

If you're in a tight spot in life, you'll be lucky if, like me, you're able to turn something you're passionate about into something that's both rewarding and lucrative. There could be all sorts of things you're thinking of – sports, architecture, upcycling Sainbury's bags for life into designer clothes – but for me, the passion that turned my life around was music.

The first time I saw someone MC, it was like the first time I'd seen a guy going backwards on rollerskates. It was *that* monumental. Now with the rollerskates, I tried that once, fell off, whacked my head and thought 'fuck that, I'll admire from a distance'. Sometimes you can see something and be content to just respect its craft. But there was something with MCing that made me think: 'I can get involved.'

The big moment came during the six-week school holiday in the summer of 2000. I was 15 and I'd been packed off to my Auntie Millie's house, and I saw my cousin NE, may he rest in peace, just freestyling with his mates and making beats on his PlayStation using the Music 2000 program that seemed to be everywhere at the time. I saw him spitting and

I thought he seemed really cool. More importantly, he was really fucking good. At the beginning I was just watching in the background, but afterwards, when all his mates had gone home, I was like: 'Go on then, cuz, let me have a go.'

Sometimes you just need to take a leap of faith. Follow your impulses.

Weird thing is, at that time in my life I hadn't really been about music. In my early teens I'd enjoyed singing and I'd entered talent contests at the local youth club singing 112's 'Only You'. I could actually sing back then but then my balls dropped, I developed too much bass, and it was game over. Beyond that I was more into the reggae artists I'd hear around the house – it spoke to my heritage where the UK rap scene just didn't at that point. Even so, I wasn't exactly a music head. Among me and my mates, being an MC wasn't even seen as being cool. (If anything it was being the DJ who was cool – at least the DJ would get all the fanny.)

But when I had a go on NE's mic, that all changed. And obviously, at first I was totally shit. But practice makes perfect. For the rest of the school holidays I was writing bars in Auntie Milly's basement, even if most of the time I was just stealing a lot of my cousin's lyrics, adding in some of my own and working it out from there. A sample of one of my own lyrics from back then: 'I'm the kind of guy, when I get physical, run up in your house, take all your Sky Digital.' My knowledge of life was a little limited.

By the end of the holidays I was back in Brixton, and I

remember at that time my mates started thinking I was on crack because all of a sudden I was back in SW9 talking about making music. They were like: 'What the fuck are you doing, talking about music? We laugh at musicians and we rob them, and after six weeks at your auntie's house you're back on the block talking about how you want to be one of them?'

Thing is, at that time I was doing alright on the street and making what seemed like a substantial amount of money. My friends couldn't understand why I'd stop doing something that was making money, or at the same time why I'd think about doing something that wouldn't make money. But I didn't listen to them. I used to write on my block, just sitting on my doorstep: a bag full of weed, some custard creams, some Happy Shopper lemonade and my notebook. And I was gradually starting to realise that I could use my bars to articulate the shit I was going through. There was a lot of shit. Imagine me at that age with no sense of life: I was bitter and angry. My highest ambition until then had been to become the biggest drug dealer in the world, and I felt that if I lived past 25 that'd be a bonus.

So I decided to combine the two. When I asked myself what I wanted to do with MCing and how I wanted to do it, I decided that I wanted to do music just like I'd done the drugs: 'I'm going to be a drug dealer of emotions. I'm going to supply free emotions. Pain. Gut-wrenching pain.' And I knew a lot about pain, so I could spit about that.

When I thought about people who might hear my words, I thought: 'If you want a track about bettering your relationship I can't help you, but if you want a track about life in a fucking shithole, maybe I can help. And if you want a song to smash the house up to, I can do that for you too.'

One big turning point was when I saw Major Ace in a rave at Chillin', the under-18s event they used to do at the Brixton Fridge. Because he had a bit of a Jamaican twang to his music, it resonated with me – it was a bridge between the music I'd grown up with, and the music I was starting to make. Another key moment was when Pastor Chris bought a set of decks and some mic equipment for the youth club, and every Monday became music night. It was just battling to start with, throwing insults at your mates and slagging each other off on the beat. Pastor Chris getting that equipment in was a really big deal. Apart from using Music 2000 on your PlayStation, music equipment was mad expensive back in those days and it wasn't like today when you can pretty much make an album on your mobile phone. So the youth club became a focal point: the whole area got involved, and after a few weeks it was like we were developing our own musical community.

Then we'd go to other places: my church youth club would battle another church youth club, and so on. I'd go to venues like Brixton Mass and Norwood Snooker Hall: you had to be a real fucking Spartan to go to these places. Normal people couldn't go, and even I'd be shitting my pants on the bus there, wondering if I'd end up walking home barefooted. Lawless. Absolutely lawless. But gradually, I felt like I was getting bigger. Something was unfolding.

It's hard sometimes to know when your life's starting to change. Easy afterwards, but in the moment you don't always notice. I definitely felt that something was shifting – you'll do better in life if you're also able to understand *in the moment* that you're finding yourself in the position to make a change.

Then there were the house parties. Not at my own house, obviously – I'm not mental. We'd find out where you were throwing a party that was going off, then we'd come in your house, try to get with a girl, smoke hella weed, shout 'BRIXTON' a lot, go on the mic, throw the mic on the floor, rob people and go home. Proper Viking style. There was one party in Norwood (no idea whose house it was, we just gatecrashed) where I got the biggest response of the night. BOOM. I absolutely fucking smashed it. There was a spark there that was setting me apart from everyone else.

That was the first time my mates had really seen me smash it in a battle, and after that my crew took shape. It was the early days of grime and we were called NAA: it was me, DJ Frampster, Dreama, Innocent, Reds, Oozy, YO, Infamous, L Man, MC Solo, Typah, Suey, Stamina, Page and Duke. I'd grown up with most of them and some I'd met through music. We played everywhere; at one point NAA had the biggest under-18s event in south London, but while we knew how to play raves and we all knew how to spit, I didn't know how to make songs and they couldn't teach me to make songs because they didn't know either.

I didn't even know what bars were! I'd just been sitting on the block with my A4 sheets of paper and when I used to go to parties I'd get in trouble for hogging. They'd be like: 'Man's hogging all the riddim.' But I didn't know about bars, so I was just like: 'I've been up all night smoking weed writing this shit, you're going to fucking listen.'

It came to the point where I realised where my limitations were. I had a choice: stay as a rave MC my entire life, or take a new direction where I could get in the studio and someone could show me how to make a song. You'll find yourself at that sort of crossroads numerous times in life, whatever you're doing with your days. The easy option is to stay where you are. The more exciting option: LEARN.

NAA's management at the time, CEO, got me in a studio session with Commander B to see what would happen. I turned out alright, considering I'd never made songs before – I was a straight up battle rapper and MC, but CEO could see that there was some potential there. He was a big brother to all of us back then and to have someone showing belief in me when I'd been told my whole life I'd go nowhere ... well, that was a big thing.

That chapter of NAA ended up coming to a natural close. Nothing can last forever and the simple fact is a lot of man had kids early. Everything could have been different if I'd had my first kid at 16 or 17 but I was fortunate that I had my kids later down, so I could focus on myself. Moving on to the next step like that, when you're in a crew that's like brothers, can involve a tough conversation or two, but if someone's your true friend it's natural that they should want you to go further in your life. It's like leaving your mum's house: if you leave after an argument with negative vibes, you won't feel comfortable going back there. If you leave with love and a good vibe your mum's house will always be your house. You can leave your mates but you just have to do it the right way, so the door is always open. I'll be NAA for life.

As time went by, more positive stuff started coming my way. Raw Materials, a community recording studio in Brixton, showed early support when they gave me 10,000 blank CDs and challenged me to fill them. It was like my first ever record deal: no cash, but the ability to get my music into 10,000 pairs of hands. My boy Suey did a DJ mix for 40 minutes and I just rapped all over it. We didn't even have CD covers; man just gave out these CDs to everyone in the local area, out on the street, at school, at house parties. Raw Material's plan was so smart: give man some money and he'll spunk it up the wall but 10,000 CDs — well, if something doesn't happen out of 10,000 CDs, maybe they're not meant to make it anyway.

It was meeting Obi and Nathan, the guys from Dice Recordings, my record label to this day, that made things shift up a gear. After I got with Dice I made my first mixtape, *I'm Better Than You*. I knocked it out in 24 hours – I already had so many lyrics scattered across all these sheets of paper. At that point my boy Obi was teaching me about how songs work: 'Stop there, that can be a hook. Stop there, that can be a verse.'

Around the same time I met a guy called Tyrone who was managing Ms Dynamite – me and my bro L Man had entered a competition Pepsi were running with Polydor Records and Ms Dynamite, being signed to Polydor, had ended up being a judge. There was a point when it looked like we might actually get a deal with Polydor, who are one of the country's biggest labels, but they backed off. I think they liked the idea of inheriting some of our hood respect but the thing is hood respect isn't something you can buy, or acquire, or absorb through osmosis if you stand near enough someone who grew up on Acre Lane. Hood respect is down to years and years of history. It's your community. It's your lifetime's work. Whether you're an MC or the local candlemaker, respect from your local area isn't down to how much money you've got; it's down to how many kids you went to school and playcentre with.

People from outside would be with me in Brixton and they'd go: 'Why do so many people stop and talk to you?'

And I'd be like: 'All their brothers are in prison with my brother. They've seen me pulling my mum's shopping trolley through the market every Saturday for the last eighteen years.'

It was Tyrone who introduced me to Naughty Boy, years before he was having hits with people like Emeli Sandé and members of One Direction. Tyrone was like: 'You're good. I've got this sick boy called Shahid; let's go and meet him and see what you can build.' I went to Naughty Boy's mum's house in Watford and had the first korma I'd ever eaten; later on he used to come to my house, and meet my mum, and smoke weed, and I introduced him to everyone in the London music scene. We ended up doing a song called 'Big Love' with Bashy and Scorcher but then … he shat on me. He distanced himself from me. We still see each other from time to time – there's no beef, but it's 'hi and goodbye' because there's nothing else to say. It's fine, and I've got no malice.

That said, he knows he's a …

Anyway, Dice changed everything, and not just for my career. I had no idea that it was happening but my mum had started phoning Obi and Nathan behind my back, begging them to get her son out of Brixton. She told them: 'There's no chance for him in Brixton.'

Real talk now, I have to take my hat off to Dice, because they knew that before they could even think about me moving ahead in music, I had to get settled. They had to take me out of the environment I'd been in my entire life. And if they hadn't done that I'd definitely be dead or doing life in prison. Without that part of the story, and without them moving me out of the fucked up environment I was in, there would be no Big Narstie. No music, no BDL, no TV. They knew I couldn't go in the studio every day knowing I'm in beef and that there's people trying to kill me. I mean, from a totally business point of view, how could they invest loads of money in someone living in a fucking warzone, not knowing if he's going to get shot the minute he comes out of his front door?

But that's the difference between Dice and a big label. If I'd been with a major, they'd have just given me loads of money and left me in Brixton to rot. That's a good lesson we could all learn something from: always look *behind* what someone's telling you. Always look at what they *really* mean.

It was when I moved to Essex that I realised something was actually happening. I had the physical space and the breathing space to actually consider that I might have a future, whereas back in the claustrophobic environment of Brixton I'd felt like at any moment everything could just go back to how it was. I remember one New Year's Eve, Obi said to me: 'You're going to be big, but it's not just going to be through your music. The people have to really understand you and when they do, the world's going to love you.'

Everything slowly started spiralling, and it looked like Obi had been right. It felt so surreal when I started getting coverage – there was one point when I got played on an

MTV Base advert every two hours, every day; I got onto Channel U and all the radio stations. My first big write-up was in RWD magazine after my Coldplay remix, 'Spun The Web', got a radio play. The write-up said: 'Grime meets indie, could this be the new awakening of grindie?' And I thought: 'What the fuck is grindie?'

The better I started doing, the more pressure there was to make sure I took it the whole way and really made it. I didn't want to be one of those MCs who got really close and didn't get there. There's nothing sadder than that. But then things got fucked up when I ended up in hospital with mould growing in my lung. After weeks out of action, the local council couldn't find me anywhere to stay and I was back in Brixton, thinking that I'd have to hit the streets again. It felt like I was totally fucked.

When I looked at getting back into music after I got out of hospital, it seemed like the whole grime scene had changed. I'd been out of the scene for over six months, which doesn't sound long but on the streets music can change a lot in that time. I remember my boy Dullah saying: 'Grime's not really how you remember it.'

I'd lost my seat.

So I had a question: do I hold onto my pride and think I'm Billy Big Bollocks just because I've got a bit of a resumé? Or do I eat a slice of humble pie and go back to the basics?

A little life rule here: humble pie doesn't always taste as bad as you think it will. So I went back to the basics. I had to take in grime all over again – the new producers, the new MCs, the new sounds. It was like I had to learn my craft from scratch. I found myself gatecrashing loads of nights. I was up and about. Wherever I could get a performance. I did nearly thirty shows for free, trying to get myself back and relevant. I had to make that investment. I had to make promoters see what would happen when I was around. I ended up standing on a stage with artists I'd been way bigger than before they were even around, and they were going: 'Hey, Narstie's here for free? That's sad.'

But I had the bigger picture in my mind. Truth be told I didn't know that the gamble was going to pay off but I wanted to prove them wrong. Their doubting made me hungry.

Now, a lot of artists will tell you that going back to basics is a liberating and exciting feeling. That's why you see huge stadium artists doing little shows in tiny pub venues: they want to recreate the feeling they once had when they were on their way up. But take it from someone who really has started again: for me, it wasn't very enjoyable. Picture it: I'm giving myself up for free, feeling like I've fucked it, and people are wondering what's going on in my head. Bleak times.

At least, to start with. But then I noticed things starting to turn around. After I'd done 27 free shows, I started getting offers for paid ones. And that was a little bit exciting. It all started snowballing. Before too long I was back on top. And it made me realise something relating to a question a lot of big artists sometimes wonder: 'If I had to do it again, could I get away with it? Or was it just luck the first time round?' Well, I did it again. And the second time round, things got even bigger than they'd been before.

Bigger, actually, than even I wanted to admit to myself. Even as recently as 2016 I was still having trouble computing just how big I'd become. I had this period of a couple of weeks when I kept getting prank calls from some bloke pretending to be Robbie Williams – it was doing my head in, and I just kept hanging up on him. Then I got a call from my booking agent, Miles, going: 'Can you please stop hanging up on Robbie Williams?' We ended up in the studio, with me smoking a mad amount of weed, recording a song called 'Go Mental' for one of his projects. He's a cool guy actually. He said he liked my music and the videos of mine that he'd seen on YouTube, and all I'm thinking is: 'Robbie Williams has Googled me – what the fuck?' When I'm not hanging up on multi-million-selling superstars I'm fortunate in that most of my collaborations seem to happen quite genuinely. Whether it's Craig David, Spice, Ed Sheeran or Fatman motherfucking Scoop, I find myself in the studio with people I really respect. I couldn't just go in a studio with a person I've never heard of before in my entire life, just because they're big. It's all about back story. And when I know that people want to work with me because of my back story, I become interested in theirs. Collaborations have to flow. They can't be forced.

I suppose it depends on what sort of music you're making but for me authenticity has to 100% be the priority – and you'll find that's true in plenty of other areas of life too. In relationships, in work, in friendships, how many times have you found that the root of a problem is something to do with a lack of authenticity?

Trouble is, when authenticity's concerned, you never know where you're going to find problems. Example: it was nice taking my mum and my missus to an award ceremony a few years back. My mum, especially, was really happy with the night out. I'd been nominated for an award and she said: 'Well done, son. I'm proud to see you doing well in your dreams.' But the night made me quite disheartened at the same time: I might have been nominated, but I'd had to pay six and a half grand (plus VAT) for the table; otherwise I'd have been sitting in the audience watching everyone else who'd been nominated against me sitting at their big tables. The price of ego? Perhaps. Mad to notice, though, that every single person who'd bought a *platinum* table package strangely seemed to win an award. Total coincidence, I'm sure.

Maybe the thing is that man suffered so long trying to get into the music industry that even when I was doing good it felt like I was suffering. Even when I won awards, I was angry. I'm still angry, really. And another thing that makes me angry about music is how a lot of old-school artists are so scared of fresh blood and talent that when they get to the top they try to pull the ladder up. That's no good at all.

Fact is, if you can swallow your pride and if you're not ignorant, you'll realise that you can learn a lot from the next generation. Mankind's ignorance is what always fucks it. I noticed that kind of behaviour a bit when I was on my own way up: I could see my forefathers trying to stop me coming through. They'd had a scene that worked; they'd been controlling it for over 25 years, they knew they'd have their annual bookings every summer, and they didn't want anyone new taking that away from them. It was like *Highlander*: they thought there could only be one.

That was part of the whole story of grime around 2004, when the entire music industry wasn't doing anything to let our music in. Worse than that, it was trying to keep grime out. The powers that be knew they didn't want a load of ghetto people getting through, because they didn't want us to be able to change our economic stature. It's easy to control poor black kids. It's not to easy to control rich black kids. But the powers that be didn't realise this: it doesn't matter how much money you have if you don't have the right mindstate. Without the right mindstate, you'll always be poor. And the kids you're trying to keep down will make their way, regardless.

That's just what happened with grime, which is now one of the biggest musical genres in the UK. Some people on the street aren't sure about how mainstream grime's got, but I think it's all good: the main thing right now is that kids who do this music have a chance of seeing a financial future from it, and that's never a bad thing. The question, though, is what the leaders at the front of the scene are doing with their position. Are they setting up the scene to be a time-limited scene, just for their era, or are they setting it up as something that can have longevity and grow roots? Are they pulling in the next generation, or pushing them back like the generation before us tried to push us back? I hope grime can have a legacy like reggae: pioneered by the leaders back in the day, but with new artists coming through all the time who are flying the flag.

I've got no time for two-facedness in the music world. What I love about the street is that if I don't like you, it's simple: I think you're a cunt, I think you're snidey and I don't want nothing to do with you. Likewise, you probably think I'm a cunt too. You stay away from me; I stay away from you. Sorted! We both know where we stand. The music industry is not like that. It's all, 'Hey, alright mate, how's the kids', then as soon as he's turned his back it's, 'I fucking hate this guy, don't work with him'. And the industry is always the same people going round and round in circles, jumping from job to job and label to label. They fuck artists, they lose their jobs, they join a new company and do the same thing all over again.

If I'd won that Ms Dynamite competition back in the day I would have signed with Polydor like a shot, but the more I've learned about the music business in the years since, the less likely I've become to sign my life away to a big company. Over the years I've had offers, but I turned down signing to major companies because I wanted control. I learned that they 'pay for say' – by that, I mean that if someone gives you half a million pounds they've paid for a say in what you're doing.

When you hear of an artist signing a million-pound record deal, the artist isn't getting the cash for no reason. It's not a present! That cash was on the table because the artist needed to be persuaded to give up their voice, and it was cash that did all the persuading. If I gave my liberty to any crazy company they could be having me doing adverts I don't want to do – ads that aren't in my moral code, or for products I don't like. Think about it: I wouldn't kiss a dog in an advert, but if someone's got half a million quid invested in me, too right they're going to force me. It's like selling shares in your own existence, and realising too late that someone else is the majority shareholder. And of course once you've kissed a dog in an advert once, you know what will happen next. They'll want you to do it again, but this time with a horse. Or a pig. Or the whole farmyard.

Obviously the other part of being on a big record label is that once they've decided you've had your day, you're out on your arse. Look at it like this: if I had a Number One song right now, all the crazy bookings would start coming in. Money being thrown at me left, right, and centre. But that's all rented. When you have success like that, you're in someone else's mainframe; you're just renting your space in it. Spots on big stages, the right producers, clothes, events, the whole thing – you're popular and you're relevant, but it's borrowed.

And then … well, when you're not Number One any more, and maybe you haven't had a Number One for a while, and perhaps your last track got 80% fewer streams, you're not as popular or as relevant and all the facilities that were at your disposal slowly start to decrease. People start edging away. It doesn't always happen overnight, either. Usually it's slow. So slow that you don't always notice it happening. You could say that the clock starts ticking as soon as you hit your peak. Problem is, most people don't realise when they've peaked. And they don't hear the ticking clock until it's too late.

As far as I can see it, the best insurance against all that is to face up to the fact that there's only one person who's never going to pull away when things get bad, and that's you. Or in my case, it's me and the mandem at Dice. If the music industry's the UK, we're like Shetland: sort of part of it, but cut off enough to just get on with our lives in peace. I'm tucked away, and I'm independent, and I'm an outsider, and I'm everything some people despise. But I'm here by popular demand, even though some people didn't want me here, thanks to Dice and the BDL army. In *Game of Thrones* terms, I'm King of the North; everyone's under the rule of the Seven Kingdoms, but the north has its own jurisdiction.

Hear this now: I didn't see really big success until the last five or six years. From 18 to my mid-twenties, how many people do you think told me to quit? They could have thought in their heart of hearts they were giving me truthful advice – I'd been doing it so long and I hadn't fully made it. They probably thought they were being helpful.

But the truth is always the best answer, and the truth here is that in life some things happen quick for some, and real slow for others. You'll probably have noticed this about your own life. And with time, you start to realise that life isn't a competition – at least, not one with a time limit.

It takes a while to accept that things will go at their own pace, though. Before I really started smashing it, I wanted to know why I hadn't been pushed ahead a little further, a little sooner. I always used to say: 'God, why did you make me blow so late?' And I still don't think I've fully blown, but what I didn't understand back in the day was that it had to take me this long to make it. It had to take all those years mingling with really rich people and really poor people; intelligent people, bland people, psychotic people, passive aggressive people, smiley-but-evil people. Straight up evil people. It took all those years, and all that shit, and the mould in my lung and all the setbacks, to finally arrive at the mindstate that would take me all the way.

None of this could have been rushed. It was always going to happen. It had to happen. But it was only ever going to happen when the time was right.

11

MIND AND BODY: LOOKING AFTER YOURSELF, INSIDE AND OUT

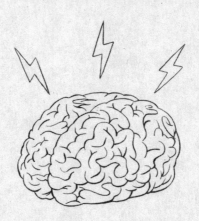

You probably spend a fair amount of time looking in the mirror before a night out, checking out your appearance and making sure you look your best. Maybe you go to the gym or get in some running each morning. But while it's common for people to pay close attention to the physical side of their well-being, I want you to pay just as close attention to what's happening inside your head.

For instance: it's alright to be sad. Not every day is going to be tea and biscuits and sunshine. But sometimes there's plenty of tea, plenty of biscuits and plenty of sunshine, and you're still sad.

Last night I was watching a film and I fell asleep on the settee. I woke up at 3 a.m. and just burst into tears. I was angry for no reason. Then I sat on the toilet seat and Googled military security for half an hour. Why was I angry? No idea. Why did I cry? Don't know. Why was I Googling military security? Fuck knows! From the outside things might seem pretty good in my life these days, but my mood doesn't always match my circumstances.

It's unusual, still, for people (especially men) to talk about their mental health. Truth be told, I wasn't fully ready to talk about it until I was in my twenties, but the more I look at my own situation, and the more I hear about what others are going through, the more I know it's something we all need to talk about a lot more.

I remember a Saturday morning when I was small, and I was walking back from Iceland with my mum, just like I did pretty much every Saturday. On the way home we saw a madman sitting outside Woolworths on Brixton high road. His behaviour seemed funny to me and I laughed and pointed at him, but my mum was having none of it. She dragged me to one side and slapped me, right there in the middle of the street. It seemed like she was angry with me in a way I hadn't seen her be angry before.

She told me: 'Don't you ever laugh at a person who's crazy. You don't know what's put them there – and you don't know what problems you might go through when you're older. There are problems in life that you can't even imagine, and they'll test your mental state.'

What she was saying didn't really make any sense to me then, but it makes more sense to me now, and I bet it makes sense to you too. After 34 years of life I've been through situations that have tested my mental stability and I just give thanks to God that I'm mentally strong enough to have come out the other end in one piece.

Any ghetto kid will grow up seeing a lot of blokes like that Woolworths guy. When you're in that sort of environment you get to know who the crackheads are, and you get to know where the madmen are. There were several schizo-phrenic people living on my street. They'd sit there with their music boxes on the doorsteps, rocking backwards and forwards, totally casual, but my mates would say to me: 'These people could kill you, then they'd be let out of the police station the next day.' I didn't understand what those people were going through, and like a lot of people who don't understand things I became fearful of them.

As I got a little bit older and was a few years into primary school, I started to get more of an idea what these people were going through. With my mum being a nurse, and what with me often having to accompany her to work before school, and then meet her again afterwards, life in what I knew as 'the madhouse' became less unusual to me. My experience of being at the hospitals was eye-opening: those guys didn't have any horrible or aggressive tenden-cies to me. They were nice, and gentle, and calm with me. But if I'm honest, I resented my mum's job a little when I was younger. How many kids do you know who spend their spare time in the madhouse, seeing men eating their own shit? I thought: 'Why do I have to do this?' When I asked my mum why these people were in the hospital, her explanation was pretty plain: 'It's simple: they're mad and they need help.'

I definitely didn't grow up thinking that what was affecting those guys in hospital was normal, but it wasn't taboo either. That was pretty fortunate, because as I went through my teens it became clear to me just how complex a thing the brain really is. And it became clear in a way that was as close to home as it's possible to be.

In my early teens I started to experience really strong, frequent emotional swings: I'd be really happy, then really sad, and whether I was happy or sad seemed to have no relation to the sort of situation I was in. So I could be in a room full of loads of people I loved at a family party, but I'd be so sad. There'd be food, there'd be music, there'd be smiling faces, but I'd just feel an emptiness that made no sense. I remember once, when my brother came out of prison for my 16th birthday, it was such a happy occasion, but I felt really desolate. And I didn't know why. It was so confusing for me. How could I feel sad, and happy, at the same time, and not be able to explain either?

People would say: 'Cheer up, it's a happy occasion.'

If you've had issues around your own mental health, or if you've known people who've struggled with theirs, you'll already know that it wasn't that simple. What made it worse was that I didn't know how to explain what I was feeling. To *anybody*. I just didn't have the words. Just as difficult was the fact that I didn't know if anyone would want to listen. It's not like saying: 'Oh, I'm sad because my friend died, my mum's ill and life's just a bit shit'. That sort of thing's just a reaction to life, right? That sort of stuff's important to be open about, obviously, but at least it's understandable: you could tell a mate and they'd be able to sympathise, or empathise, or at least make some sort of sense of what you were going through.

When you feel sad and you don't want to get up and don't know why, that's a different matter. These terrible, dark, down moments, where I'd have no energy, would continue to pop up throughout my teens and into my twenties. I hated life, I hated myself. There were times when I even thought about suicide. I suppose loads of people have thought about it at one time or another: they've thought about getting out of this fucking world. And I guess the thing is, thoughts are thoughts, and I'm so grateful that's all they were with me – even in my darkest hours I still felt that I had more to live for than I did to go for. But that's not to say those thoughts didn't go deep at the time.

I went to the doctor and told them that I was feeling really low, and really down, in an unexplainable way. I was in my early twenties by this point and I'd been feeling this way since my teens – it had taken a lot of time for me to get together the courage to go to them and say: 'I'm feeling weird, and I don't know why.'

After I'd done my best to explain my situation, I told man to please be honest with me about what I should do next. His words will always stay with me: 'Have some fucking tablets, bruv, and get your fucking mind back.'

Literally, word for word, that's what he said. Get. Your. Fucking. Mind. Back.

His solution was to prescribe me some Cipramil. A 'selective serotonin reuptake inhibitor', apparently. An anti-depressant, to you and me. Or as my not-very-helpful mates would have called them at the time: 'madmen tablets'.

I don't really blame the doctor because I know doctors train for a long time and it's like 'if someone comes to you with this, give them that', and I know policies change from time to time in the NHS. For instance, these days I think doctors are less likely to just give you a load of pills, and they're more likely to put you on a waiting list for counselling. But anyway, my experience was that if you go to the doctor and open your heart to them, and they just give you pills, it's like you're not being listened to. You're not being heard.

I went and got the prescription, but when I told my family they were like: 'Don't you ever fucking take them tablets.' They went straight down the toilet.

I don't know how I feel about that advice. I was blessed that having taken the step of opening up to my doctor I then felt that I could be more open about my situation with some members of my family and I had a great support system with my mates, which ended up being my own substitute for counselling. To someone who doesn't have that support system, and can't be open with their friends or family, that support system has to be what they're being offered by their doctor, whether it's counselling, medication or something else. I'd say this to everyone: use the facilities that are within your reach. If it's family and friends, great. If it's just medication, great. If it's family and friends *and* medication, and if that feels right for you, do that too. Do what you need to do so you can ... well, in my doctor's words, get your fucking mind back.

If the idea of opening up to your mates seems scary, I understand. But I want you to understand this: some of them might just surprise you. You need your mates around you, man. You might think that it's hard to change the vibe if your friendships are just banter, but think about it another way: if it's usually about banter, that might actually make it easier to change the tone, and to have a meaningful dialogue with people. With me, it's obvious that banter is my natural demeanour and that means that when I do change, and when I'm having dark thoughts, it's very obvious to my close circuit that I'm not myself. It's like with my missus, who's been with me long enough to notice something's up as soon as I walk through the door. I don't need to say anything and she knows something's up. Same with my mates.

When that does happen and it's obvious something's wrong, it's when you find out who your mates are – and I mean your *real* mates. You can have a lot of people around you in life, but that doesn't make it a support system. A real support system is made up of people who genuinely check for you: people who like hanging out with you and having fun, but who also hang around when you're not fun.

Last year when my daughter started school for the first day it hit me harder than I could ever have imagined. My little girl was growing up, and I was an emotional wreck. I tweeted a message going: 'This thing's fucked me up more than I thought it would – I'm on the ropes.' Five of my friends were immediately there in my WhatsApp, checking in on me, asking how she was doing, offering to meet up.

In my down moments, I'm lucky that I have good people around me; there'll be man going: 'Shut up, you fat sweat. Let's play FIFA.' And what man's doing isn't just wanting to play FIFA, he's wanting me to know he's there for me. And I know that if and when I'm ready, I can put down my controller and go: 'You know what, cuz, I'm fucking stressed out. I want to fucking kill everyone and I hate this life.'

As well as having mates who are aware of *your* well-being, it's important that you keep an eye on how your own mates are. If they're quiet, maybe there's something going on. If they keep cancelling on you, maybe they're not being a dick – maybe they're not alright. Everyone has their moments. Sometimes you just need someone to listen and not say anything – you need to feel heard and that people are taking you seriously. And sometimes … well, sometimes it's you who needs to do the listening.

Listening isn't just about words. They say that 93% of communication is non-verbal: it's about expressions, and body language, and all that stuff you only get from being in the same room as someone.

The good thing for me is that my relationship with my friends and my close circuit isn't a mobile phone relationship. There's none of that 'I'll text to see if you're in' business – if I'm driving past your house I'll just knock on your door. Real human interaction is the key, even in these times of WhatsApp and instant messaging. *Especially* now. If you've just broken up with your other half and you're texting me telling me everything's okay, with a little smiley emoji at the end, I'm not taking that as the answer – I'm coming round your place to look you in the eye and to see if you're really okay. When you look into a person's face and speak to them, it's different. Maybe someone just needs a fucking hug. You can't go wrong with a hug. And for that you need face-to-face time, not FaceTime.

It's not always easy to talk, though, even with friends. It's no secret, for instance, that in Jamaican communities, discussion of mental health is very stigmatised. It's often the case that they'll try to put people who are 'crazy' – that catch-all term for any number of mental health issues and development disorders – to the back of their minds, or the back of their houses, as dirty secrets. It all comes back to that idea that people are scared of what they don't understand. Cousin Gary might be autistic, but they go: 'Gary's mad, keep him in his room.' Auntie Mabel might be depressed, and it's: 'Don't let her come to the next family party.'

I used to think this was just something to do with my local community back in Brixton, but when I did some speaking dates with the mental health charity MIND, I realised the real extent of Caribbean culture's reluctance to really go in on mental health. When I was in Sheffield, a girl was telling me about her uncle. For the longest time her family had always played down his issues, claiming he didn't have a problem – but they kept him hushed up in the corner of their house. It was only when she got to university and invited her friends round that they said: 'Hang on, your uncle's fucking nuts.' Hiding him away from the wider world, and even hiding him away from his own issues, hadn't helped anyone – least of all him, and he was the one who needed the help. Until this girl intervened, he'd been experiencing the very worst of the world.

I've been lucky that my own family have been a little more open-minded, particularly in recent years when I've explored what it means to be bipolar, and I've come to the conclusion that it's something that's impacting my own life. Before I considered that I might be bipolar, I'd already got to the point where I was talking about mental health with a lot of people through my work, because I was feeling strongly about it and thought it was important to share my own experiences, but it was only when I heard other people talking about bipolar that I started to recognise my own experiences in what I was hearing.

As I've learned more about mental health, both from my own perspective and from what mates have been telling me, I've realised that we all need to be a lot more mindful of what's happening behind the exteriors we show the world. I feel guilty about that five-year-old version of me, laughing at some geezer outside Woolworths, and I know now that we'll all meet all sorts of different people, and they'll each be at very different stages of their mental health journeys. Take my mate, for instance – he's done so much prison time that he's only comfortable in small spaces. He's agoraphobic: there's a postbox near to his house, and, if he goes past it, he'll collapse. He's got a flash car and he can never use it.

Now obviously, looking after your mind is just one part of looking after yourself. There's no getting around the fact that I'm not exactly in possession of a six-pack and bulging biceps. Some fat people don't like being called fat. They think of themselves as 'bigger', or they prefer to be referred to as 'overweight'. Some of them even think 'overweight' isn't politically correct, and I understand why they might want to get away from words that make them feel bad about themselves. But, as far as I'm concerned, I'm fat.

To be more specific: I'm a fat cunt. Every human being on the face of this planet is one of two types of cunt; you're either a skinny cunt or a fat cunt, and I'm the latter. (Take the T-shirt test to find out which you are – skinny cunts take an S, an M, an L, and maybe they're even scraping into XL territory. Fat cunts like me are XXL, XXXL and above – all the fucking Xs. It's very simple.)

But don't think that just because I'm a fat cunt I don't love myself. As far as I'm concerned, of all the things people have used against me in the past or shouted at me about in the street – I'm fat, I'm short, I'm black – there's nothing wrong with any of it. I'll put it another way. Think how ridiculous I'd look if I was skinny, and if I started wearing medium size T-shirts. I'd look wrong! I'd look like a fucking crackhead. Small Narstie wouldn't work. Medium Narstie just wouldn't cut it. I'm Big Narstie, and I need to be big.

I've always been big and it never used to trouble me, even at school. I just got on with life, and didn't make any excuses. How could I? I couldn't say to my cousin: 'I'm not coming to Streatham Megabowl with you on my bike, I'm a bit bigger than you and I can't ride.' I couldn't say: 'I'm not climbing that tree because I'm fat.' My mates would have called me a fucking knob; I'd have got my arse whooped – and quite right too. None of us put up with any health-related excuses when we were kids. My cousin Kwesi had a serious disease and it was so bad he couldn't even go to school as a kid, but me and his other cousins all gave him a fucking dead leg whenever we saw him, just as we did for everyone else.

I think that as soon as you start playing on one hindrance in your life and thinking everything should be special for you, you've lost. Life just doesn't work like that – instead, you have to work with your hindrances and just *cut forward*. I did the mountain bike ride from Brixton to Streatham with my mates. I climbed the trees, too. It might have taken me a bit longer to climb them but I got scratches on my leg like everyone else, and I enjoyed myself like everyone else, and in the end I got to the top of the tree like everyone else.

Loads of guys think they need to get ripped to pick up girls, but in my experience that wasn't necessary. I always got quite enough pussy, thanks very much – I found out early that girls aren't as shallow as guys are, and a six-pack wouldn't have got me any more pussy than I already got.

That said, a couple of years back I did have to confront some of my body's limitations. I'd been invited to take part on a celebrity version of the *Great British Bake Off* along with people like Rylan, Johnny Vegas and Russell Brand. I stormed through the first day of filming, turning out these banging Big Dog shortbreads – they might not have had the best look, and actually they looked fucking awful, but taste-wise I absolutely shat on everyone else. They tasted better than everyone else's shortbreads, even Prue Leith agreed! The salted caramel dollops on top conveyed a serious message, too: pick up after your animals.

But when I got back to my hotel that night, I wasn't feeling right. I started seriously flaking out; I felt like my whole body was going weird. Next thing I knew, I was on the floor, calling for my boy Caspar C to drive me to hospital.

It was only when the doctor asked me what I'd been doing recently to cause the collapse that I realised how packed my diary had been. I'd been on the go nine days straight with what must have been about 24 hours' sleep in that whole time; right before *Bake Off*, I'd done six shows in two days.

I should never have done *Bake Off*. I'd run myself into the ground, and in the end my body had just had enough.

By that point in my life, I'd become pretty good at paying attention to my mental state, but that whole episode was a wake-up call for me, telling me that I should listen to what my body was telling me as well. (Real talk now: listen to your body.) Since then I've been a lot stricter with myself: no more burning the candle at both ends, and when I'm tired I sleep. I had to be more ruthless with how I spent my time, but I found that even if I spent less time doing things I became more productive when I *was* doing something. I realised there's no point trying to stay awake and get things done if the result of that is that the next day is spent not being able to do anything. Sometimes you need to tell yourself: 'You can't do everything. You can't *be* everything. Tomorrow's another day.'

One thing I have made time for over the last couple of years has been more fitness and training. Part of the reason is that I saw how my dad had ended his days, withering away and dying, and I thought: 'I don't want to end up like that.' But I've also got into mixed martial arts, and while you need to use your brain to fight – it's like a chess game – you've also got to be fit to do what your brain wants you to do. If I'd got into martial arts or boxing earlier on, and stuck it out, I'd definitely have been on more of a healthy track in my teens, so I'm a little bit pissed I didn't tap into my fighting energy from early.

I knew I needed to start going to the gym to get my strength up for the MMA, but the first one I went to I didn't like the vibe: it was a proper macho man gym with everyone glugging away on protein shakes in their little vest tops. I mean, the place was wall-to-wall wankers, so I walked straight out. The next one I found was a quiet gym with a relaxed vibe, and that suited me down to the ground. But there aren't many decent gyms like that around, which is why I've bought a gym up in north London, and I've added a CBD centre so that once you've finished your training you can have some CBD and recover. It's called Muscle Base so you can see why the name appealed to me.

I don't think I'll ever be thin. I've still got a sweet tooth and I still love food, and if I could keep my size and still be healthy inside that'd be fine. If it's all green and lovely inside, I'm not bothered about how I look. Having said that, I've noticed in a couple of pictures recently that I've lost a bit of weight. And it feels pretty good, truth be told. Not just because I want to make sure I'm physically fit enough to punch your head in for 40 minutes, but because I've even started feeling better walking up stairs. It's been better for my family life, too, I won't lie. You don't want to be that dad at the park (and we've all seen him), sitting on a park bench like a fat sweat while his kids beg him to join in with their games.

Another upshot of my MMA training has been that I had to stop drinking. Back in the day I was a total binge drinker: I could go without a drink for ages, but then it'd come to the night of a show and I'd get absolutely shit-faced, and then I'd spend the next few days feeling totally destroyed. To start off with, the fighting training sessions were absolutely killing me if they came within a few days of a show, and my trainer was like: 'You can drink or you can smoke, it's one or the other, but if you keep doing both you'll get nowhere.' Considering I never really drank at home – I didn't exactly get to my place and kick back with a glass of wine or some Henny – and considering the fact I'm not giving up my weed for fucking anything, it was a pretty easy decision for me to make. I used to drink at shows, and now I don't, and that's that. In fact, I haven't touched a drop of booze in nearly three years. If you're thinking of cutting down or stopping drinking you probably think it's going to be impossible to knock it on the head, but without wanting to diminish the struggles a full-on alcoholic might have with booze, if things are more under control for you I think you'd be surprised how easy it can be.

I'd say my mental well-being has definitely been given a boost by the combination of knocking the booze on the head and getting fitter. It also gives me a bit of headspace. When I'm training or in the gym, I leave my phone in my bag, and it's one of the only times I'm not constantly being reminded of messages, mails, calls and all the other nonsense that lives inside my phone. You can't go wrong with that rare feeling of isolated thought: a bit of time and space to think.

I've even got into cupping therapy – it's fair to say it's not for everyone, but basically you lie down, they make a couple of tiny holes in your skin, then place little cups on top and use them to suck out … well, it sucks out all sorts of disgusting shit, I'm not going to lie. The idea behind it is that pissing, shitting and sweating alone isn't going to get everything bad out of your body, and fair play there is a LOT of fucked up stuff, like jelly, coming out of my body when I have my cupping done.

Now obviously, if you'd told me when I was 15 that one day I'd be paying good money to have some geezer slapping cups on my back so he could suck out blood and gore, I'd have told you to fuck off – but here we are. The point being that you never know what might work for you. Being in touch with who you are is the first step to being in touch with your mental health. That's the real shit right there: if you don't know yourself, how can you go out into the world? To any person suffering from mental health problems, I always say: don't look on what you're going through as a bad thing. The mind is a fragile and delicate object and sometimes when it's not working properly it just needs a bit of care and attention. I know fellas who spend more time and attention keeping their trainers looking box fresh than they do on their mental well-being.

And if other people are making your life difficult? Here's the thing. Here's the *absolute thing*. NOT EVERYBODY HAS TO MOTHERFUCKING LIKE YOU. Don't spend your time on people who make you feel bad. Whoever's meant to like you will like you. All you can do is make sure that anyone who does like you likes you for *you*. Likes you because you don't like to talk a lot, or because you talk a load. Likes you for being weird, normal, educated or an idiot. I mean, I know a few people who can be any of those things, depending on what mood they're in. There's people for everyone. As long as you're satisfied with who *you* are, and as long as you love yourself, you'll attract the right people with the right energy. As long as you can live your life without making other people's lives shit, you're good.

12

RELATIONSHIPS: WORTH THE BALL-ACHE

Truth is, relationships are hard, man. And the secret to a long one – at least a long one you want to *stay* in – is to find someone who accepts you fully for who you are, and yeah, I'm afraid that means you need to find someone who accepts your flaws along with all your good stuff. Don't look for someone who's only going to fall in love with the perfect side of you. Find someone who understands your fucked up side too.

The even trickier bit? It's not a one-way street, bruv – you need to accept the other person's fucked up side too. It's never going to be a bed of roses all the time, and some nights you won't even have any sort of bed, because you'll be sleeping on the sofa. But some of us spend so long looking for the perfect partner that we forget no human can ever be perfect. Irony is, our 'perfect partner' never *will* be perfect – but they'll be right for us, and we'll be right for them.

Here's an example of how you know when you've found the right partner. A while back, in 2017, I was booked to perform at the UK Porn Awards. When I told my mates about it, they all obviously wanted to come along, but while I'd told my missus all about it – 'Baby, I'm performing at the Porn Awards, it's going off' – and I was excited off my fucking rocker so I was talking about it with her for weeks up front, none of my mates had told their girlfriends about it. In fact, they'd all made up something else that they'd said they were doing that night. 'Just a quiet night out with a couple of mates, sweetheart' – that sort of thing.

So the day of the event rolls around and it's basically a Playboy show mixed with the last days of Rome – booze everywhere, tits everywhere, cocks everywhere. The whole thing was popping OFF. And of course, what with it being 2017, they're promoting it hard on every social network you can imagine as well as a few you've probably never heard of. Blanket coverage – and that's before you factor in the porn stars themselves, and loads of them had millions of Instagram followers. Insta's going off, Twitter's going off. And all around me I could see bare guys with their phones blowing up. Five minutes later you see them sloping out with The Head of Shame.

We've all seen The Head of Shame, and a few of us have done it ourselves from time to time. It's hanging a bit lower, isn't it, your head, when you've just been bollocked and you know they've got you banged to rights. Obviously my mates' partners saw the posts across all the socials; *obviously* my mates were getting it in the ear. 'You lied! You said you were going somewhere else!'

They'd all looked like they were trying to cover something up! As for me? Mate, I had a great time. Boobs in my face, lap dances, the whole shebang: I even had a race down Oxford Street, drunk out of my nut, with 15 porn stars, and I made the police be our referees. A truly epic night, and at the end of it I came home, showed my missus the pictures and slept perfectly. And, unlike my mates, I was sleeping in my own bed, not in the spare room.

The whole relationships thing isn't something you ever really worry about for your first few years of existence, but once puberty hits, that's it: you're gone forever. I can only offer personal insight from the male perspective but it's no secret that puberty is a total fucker for everyone on the planet, and if you're going through it now just hold on tight, grit your teeth and it'll all be over soon.

I was really embarrassed talking about it at the time but I can say it now: puberty came late for me, and it was a constant headache. It felt like all I'd hear at school was 'Jeff's got four pubes! His beard's coming through!', and then there's me, little Tyrone, waiting yonks to get a little bit of bumfluff on his face. As for downstairs – well, I had a little baby's cock until my mid-teens and on the pubes front I was rubbing mud and dirt from the garden into my pants area from the age of 11, for reasons I now don't really understand and which have absolutely no medical foundation. It wasn't until I was 14 that anything sprouted. I can't offer much medical advice, but I can tell you this: mate, if you're currently rubbing soil into your groin, give it a rest. As the old song says, you can't hurry love, and you can't hurry pubes either.

Back then I felt like there was something wrong and different about me, because my body was taking longer than Jeff's and almost everybody else's. (It was even later before I had my first wet dream – that didn't come until I was 15. It scared the shit out of me and I thought I was going to die! It felt like the end of days!) But now I realise it's just the essence of life: we're all different, and things happen to different people at different stages. If we could plan and choose everything that happened to us, life wouldn't be life any more.

Even though I didn't have a wet dream until later on, I'd actually lost my virginity – sort of – a lot earlier. Truth be told, I was just eight years old. It just sort of happened, one afternoon, in my front room. Obviously, I didn't know what I was doing with my little pecker; this silly little cocktail weenie between my legs. But as soon as I felt the intergalactic warmness of the vagina, that fuzzy temptress, I was broken. I didn't finish, and I cried afterwards.

I mean, I know crying after sex is generally a bit of a mood-killer, but the older I get the more I think: that situation was weird and not normal. I was eight years old – all I was really interested in was watching Wrestlemania smackdowns on TV. I don't remember thinking about it much afterwards, but I wonder if it affected me more than I realised at the time.

On the other hand, if I'd been 16 and I'd met a woman twice my age ... well, it would have been a different story. And I can tell you that with 100% certainty because by the time I was 16 I was basically fucking the daughters of all my mum's friends. (Mum, if you're reading this, I'm sorry!) My mum's friend would come over, and if they just so happened to have a daughter my age we'd go and play mums and dads. Oh yes: I was totally on that shit. If you're wondering what my mum thought about all this, I can tell you that she didn't fucking know a bit of it. I mean, it's not like she was standing in the corner going, 'Go on son, smash' – she's a religious woman and she'd have battered me. There was no parental guidance here. This was all under the radar, *Tom Clancy Splinter Cell* scenes. I was going across enemy lines and making it back. I was paratrooping. Also: I was a dirty little shit.

The sensation of coming was what had changed it all, and those shivers of life were everything. Plus the thing is, I just loved breasts. I still do. Just thinking of them now makes me happy. And the thing is, I'm equal opportunities on this front because I can appreciate every breast for what it is. Big breasts with little nipples, tiny titties with huge nipples like wine gums – I respect them all.

I didn't really have a girlfriend until later down the line, by the time I was about 18. Sex and relationships weren't particularly talked about in the house when I was growing up and I didn't really talk about my feelings with my parents, although I do remember feeling that I had a pretty open relationship with my mum, which meant I could tell her stuff if I needed to. It's just that she'd never have started the conversation.

One conversation I definitely started myself was when I first caught the clap and had what is known among medical professionals as a custard cock. The entire thing was freaking me out – so much so that I ran into the bathroom while my mum was showering, and started shouting: 'MUM! MY COCK IS LEAKING MAD STUFF! I DON'T KNOW WHY AND I'M SCARED!'

I ended up dangling my foreskin in front of her face, saying: 'This ain't looking too healthy, I need help.'

Her response: 'What is THIS?'

I explained to her that I'd had sex, that the day after it had been burning when I went for a piss, and that today it looked like this. It was all fucked up. I thought that was the end of me. She said: 'You're not going to die, but that's what you get for having unprotected sex.' Which didn't feel very sympathetic at the time, but looking back on it now she had a point. Learnings here: wear a condom; communicate with your mum.

Anyway, my cousin Jermaine took me to the clinic at St Thomas' Hospital near Waterloo in London, just up the road from the Florence Nightingale museum. I wonder what the OG lady with the lamp would have made of a teenage me screaming the house down while some geezer in a white coat shoved some awful contraption down the end of my cock? I doubt she'd have been very impressed with the whole situation, to be honest, although I suppose she spent enough time with soldiers to have seen far worse.

One thing that did surprise me about the whole sorry episode was the waiting room. My first impression was that there were a lot of sexy women in there, which felt unfair to me because obviously the only reason they're in there is that they've got the clap. They were off-limits, even though they were fucking fresh. But then I noticed something else – I was expecting it'd be full of shifty toerags like me, but the entire place was full of grown-ups.

Some people don't learn. But I definitely learned my own lesson that day, and I was careful after that. That was quite enough bio-warfare for me. I came out the safe side; some people don't return. It could have been something a lot stronger than the clap. Real shit.

Although I didn't really talk with my mum about sex – unless I thought my cock was going to explode – it felt easier to talk with her about the more romantic side of things. When I got my first girlfriend, this girl who called herself Legs, I remember saying to my mum: 'I want you to meet my girlfriend, I really love her.'

She just laughed: 'It's not love.'

'But I really, really care for her!'

'Not love. Love doesn't come at first sight – love comes with time and experience. Anything else is just infatuation.'

Obviously, as per fucking usual, my mum was right. You'll find lots of times in life when you get love confused with infatuation, and that's all part of growing up, but knowing there's a difference between the two is important no matter how old you are. And for me, real love didn't come until a little later on.

When I was in my late teens I used to hang out at a youth centre just off Kings Avenue in Brixton – there was this guy called Buster who'd teach the locals about making music, and one of the other kids in this class was a woman who'd go on to become a successful DJ who played in even more countries than I did. But more importantly (to me, anyway), this was also the woman I'd end up spending the rest of my life with.

Except for an excruciatingly long time she was having absolutely none of my bullshit.

As soon as I met her I had a massive crush on her, and it wasn't long before I knew she was special. She was real serious, but mad funny at the same time, and she acted like a naturally cautious person, which was the total opposite of where I was at that point in my life. And while I was loud and outgoing and sociable, she seemed super antisocial – not exactly a people person. People used to say that getting to know her was like accepting a challenge.

For me, the challenge was bigger than for everyone else. I didn't realise until I'd tried chatting her up that my reputation had preceded me. She'd been told not to fuck around with me – she was told I was bad, and that I was untrust-worthy. Apparently literally everyone was telling her that. I had a really bad reputation at the time, and so of course she was very cautious of me; she'd heard about me with other girls, and her friends had obviously told her not to go anywhere near me. To be fair to her mates, with the benefit of hindsight I can see that they had a point.

At that time in my life I had two mobile phones (and back then any guy with two mobile phones was definitely up to no good in one way or another), and I was making do with having the numbers of eight or nine girls who were just in my life to suck dick and fuck me and my friends. A pretty shit attitude on my part although I guess you could say I got what I deserved: more than once I met with girls who'd flirt with me and get me to take them back to my place. They'd make me take them to my room, but they'd also leave the front door open so that, when we were banging, their mates could come in and rob the place. They'd set me up! So I was suspicious of women, and women were suspicious of me, and my missus was being told to leave me well alone.

I suppose what her mates didn't know was that I felt differently about this one. I was knocked out by her demean-our and how she carried herself, but I wasn't exactly on the receiving end of the best of it. I had long hair back then, and when I was using the recording studio near her house, Raw Material on Robsart Street, I'd ask her to come in and plait my hair for me. I mean, I was trying to get in. It was all a ruse. And not a very successful one.

'I know about you,' she'd say. 'You're a fucking dog.'

I wasn't really in any position to argue. Until I met my missus, romance and all that side of stuff was just nowhere in my criteria. I'd been more interested in guns and drugs, and the idea of a steady relationship seemed so far away. But once I met her, I felt my priorities slowly shifting. And so, my behaviour started to change too.

I showed her I was serious by doing something I never really did with girls: I chilled with her. We watched TV and did normal stuff. She was so different from me: she was quiet, she didn't drink, she didn't smoke. And I didn't want to lie to her or be fake. I was honest with her about what was happening in my life, and what challenges I was facing. Eventually it proved to be a matter of letting time take its course, and at long last we started dating properly. Many years and two children later, we're still together.

As you can see, me putting in that time showed her, I suppose, that I wasn't just in it for one thing. Those times we spent chilling and getting to know each other, before the relationship went any further, meant that when we did start our relationship it had solid foundations. And if you can't banter in a relationship, what's the point?

I mean, I love sex, but after 45 minutes I need a recharge. What am I going to do in that time – just be quiet until we go again? No! Banter has to be a part of *all* parts of a relationship. I remember when we first moved up to Essex in our first gaff we had no TV. Well, we had a TV, but nothing was happening: there was no Netflix back then and man's from the ghetto where every single TV has a wire coat hanger stuck in the back – I'd never had an aerial in my TV, so when we first moved I didn't know how the fucking thing worked and the old coat hanger trick wasn't working. Long story short we had no TV in the middle of the World Cup! The internet hadn't even been connected at that point, and back then smartphones weren't what they are today, so all we could do was just talk and vibe and play cards.

And do you know what? It worked out fine. That should be the test for any couple moving in together. Spend the first week with no furniture and everything unplugged, and see how you go. If you're still together after seven days, you're safe to go to Ikea. (And if you're still a couple when you've finished in Ikea, you might as well get married.)

I suppose by that point in a relationship you'll probably already have met your other half's family, and I really have very little advice to give on your in-laws because, let's face it, every family is totally fucking crazy in totally different ways and you just need to accept family differences.

For instance, my missus didn't grow up like me – her family life was very reserved. In my family, every home is open to everyone; we don't phone to see who's in, we just turn up. We don't ask for a drink, we just go straight to the fridge and, while we're there, we'll probably grab a handful of food too. I didn't realise all families weren't like that until one day when my cousins turned up at the house and I wasn't there – and my missus wouldn't let them in! Being my family, they just barged their way in anyway and went straight to the fridge. As you'd expect, when I got home, the missus was having a total shitfit. We had to talk about how different our families were, and now she's fine with popping in on my family unexpected. It's a two-way street though – when I'm thinking of dropping in on her family I'll always phone ahead, and if I want something from the fridge I'll always ask first.

You need to respect where other people's lines are – and accept that the lines you've drawn yourself might seem strange to another family. But another thing I've learned is that you shouldn't always take the side of your own family. One time my little sister was rude to my missus, and I made her apologise instantly! If my mum, miraculously, was rude to my other half, I'd have to tell her it wasn't right. There can't be double standards. You need to go by the simple ethics of asking yourself who's being a fucking cunt at the time.

My missus has seen me at my highest, doing super-well, but she's seen me at my lowest as well – and to begin with I was surprised by just how open I was to showing I was vulnerable in front of another person. So much of my life was all about trying to prove who has the largest bollocks and who's the biggest dog on the block, but having a long-term partner has showed me that sometimes courage is all about being big enough to admit when you're weak. And when I was weak, she looked after me.

Truth be told, even though we've been together all this time, it still doesn't feel like I've been with her for a long time. It's mad. She's my bredrin' – and I know that beyond all the usual relationship stuff, I've got a real friend. None of that would have come my way if I hadn't shown her, in the earliest stages of getting to know her, who I really was.

That's why it's so important, when it comes to dating, to start as you mean to go on. Man's not going on Tinder saying they've got a 28-foot dong because you know that when it comes to the crunch you'll get found out, and that's exactly the same with the rest of the dating thing. Putting your best foot forward is one thing, but ultimately a date will only really work and turn into something more than a handjob round the back of Greggs if you've put your *honest* foot forward.

The reason my missus has had the pleasure of seeing my face for so many years is that whether it's the Porn Awards or a trip to Asda I can be 100% myself in front of her, and I always have been. That's the truth and you can't rob me for that. Point is: honest foot forward.

Same when it comes to dating. By all means go somewhere nice for dinner – but don't pick the fanciest restaurant in town if you can't afford to go there regularly. Do stuff that's genuine to you. Make sure you're real, make sure you be yourself. Accept that you're made up of your good self and your bad self, and that other people are made up the same way.

If you truly know yourself, that also makes it easier to *stay* yourself. How many times have you heard someone say this: 'You're not the person I first met'? Maybe you're the one who's said it! Truth be told, after a while in a relationship you start to lose little pieces of yourself, and at the same time your other half's probably losing part of themselves too. The relationship ends up being two people who hardly recognise each other – because neither is the person they first met. You find yourself losing the parts of you that they liked. You become less like the person they met in the Costa, or the park, who had different dreams, thoughts, ambitions and passions. After six or seven years the person in the park has disappeared and just turned into a walking 'I love you' robot. There's nothing special about that, and there's nothing sexy about that either.

This is only something you notice when you're in your first big relationship and you're living together – you're in each other's faces every five minutes, so what is there to talk about? You can't ask someone what they did yesterday. You were fucking WITH them yesterday!

A lot of people feel that because they're in a relationship they've got to be together all the time, but having your own space in a relationship's important. For instance, I'm not always home because I'm away so much with work, so when I do stop home for a few days we've actually got stuff to talk about. The question, 'How's things?', leads to a genuine conversation because it's a genuine question. A lot of relationships fail because people don't give each other the chance to miss each other.

Again, it comes back to independence, and there's a balancing act between being straightforward with someone, while also keeping something back for yourself. Think about it like this: you think there's two people in a relationship, but actually there's four. For each person, there's the 'relationship' person as well as the person they were before the relationship started. Your psyche is broken down in two: BOOM! If I cancel all of me, and everything that makes me Tyrone Lindo, and put everything into being a partner and a dad, I become nothing. I don't exist. A good relationship can change you and make you a better version of yourself, but all too often people lose parts of themselves so that it's no longer two individuals in a relationship.

And we've all seen this when one of our mates has suddenly come out of a relationship, right? I've had mates who've been in long relationships and when it all goes tits up they don't know if they like scrambled eggs or fried eggs. They've been so far up their missus' arse that they don't even know what they like for their own breakfast. It sounds stupid, but they've lost their identity. They don't remember playing football or going to the park with their mates, and they've dropped out on all their friends because those mates have been a 'wrong influence'. All of a sudden they're reappearing and trying to get back into society like a fucking gopher sticking its head out of the mud hole.

So keeping hold of who you are – and keeping hold of your mates – is a big part of making a relationship work, and that also means letting your partner hang out with their own mates. I've seen fellas outright BANNING their girlfriends from seeing their friends, which makes no sense to me at all. There's no reason your missus shouldn't be able to talk to her schoolmates. And anyway, do you want to talk to your missus every fucking day by yourself? Mate! And how about this: introduce your missus to your friends, too! Unless your mates are fucking your missus and you need to keep them separate, one shouldn't replace the other.

That's why I say independence is so important in a relationship. There's an unwritten rule in my house: I only spend three to four days, max, in my house with my family. After that I fuck off, I go wherever I want to go, I get my work done. There's a full fucking fridge, the mortgage is perfectly in order, nobody needs anything and after four days I'm going to go and do what I need to do.

The funny thing is, the more independent you are, the stronger your relationship can become. So with me, I can cook, I can clean, I know how the washing machine works and I've got a fat bank account. My missus knows I'm with her because I love her, not because she'll wash my clothes or cook my food, or because I need her financial support, or because I don't know where my pants are. I've got mates whose birds go away on holiday for a fortnight and within five days they're living like fucking hobos: no fresh clothes, takeaway boxes piling up, the whole nine yards. They're living like children. I'm sorry but if you're a bloke and you don't know how to turn the big knob to 'J' (or whatever the setting is on your washing machine) and do an economy wash, you're a fucking twat and you don't deserve a girlfriend.

Sometimes all it comes to down with relationships is keeping in mind that humans are social creatures. If you don't feel feel comfortable in your environment you'll end up trying to find an environment where you CAN be comfortable. And after a bit of trial and error, you find it.

Sometimes I'll be out shopping with my missus and I'll be like: 'Babe, look at the arse on that woman.'

Her response is usually quite simple: 'You're an idiot.'

Spot on, obviously. But I'm not just any idiot; I'm *her* idiot.

13

LIFE AND DEATH: HOW TO NAVIGATE IT

You'll find that plenty of people will talk to you about life and death, but I'm one of the only people you'll meet with first-hand experience of both. Which is to say, I'm alive, but I've also died. And yeah, it does my head in too. Long story short, when I first moved to Essex and the mould-infested flat tried to kill me, I passed out and collapsed. I remember being in an ambulance, unable to breathe, but after that there's just black. The next thing I remember is being in the hospital, jolting forward with a fat needle in my chest: proper *Pulp Fiction* shit. The doctors told me I'd been dead for a minute before I'd exploded back to life.

I've dealt out some common sense statements in this book so far but here's the most no-shit-Sherlock thing you'll ever read: there's something about dying that makes you appreciate life a little bit more. And after you've been recovering in a hospital bed for three months, like I did, and you get to come out and walk down Brixton high road, that same high road you've walked down a thousand times seems different. To everyone else it might be the same shitty high road but to you it's magical. The air tastes different.

All senses are just heightened. Real talk: you truly appreciate life once you've seen its real essence.

It was a few years after that when I was forced to confront both life and death in one amazing, terrible moment. I'll spare you the full details but long story short when she was pregnant for our first child, my missus developed pre-eclampsia, a medical condition that affects pregnant women and whose effects range from the mild to the severe. On this case, it was severe. She gave birth to my daughter during an epileptic fit.

During the birth I genuinely thought my partner was going to die, and the medics weren't giving me much hope that things would turn out well. It was a variety of emotions, to put it mildly: I'd just become the father of a beautiful kid, but I didn't know the kid yet; and my missus, who I'd known for over a decade, looked like she was about to die, so I didn't know where to put my attention. I saw my daughter lying on a little silver table unattended while the medics ran around trying to save my missus. I felt like I was either a single parent or likely to become one. It was REAL shit. It rocked my mind. I was trying to celebrate the new life that had come into the world, except I couldn't help but think about what was happening to my missus and also, therefore, what happens at the end of life. I was thinking of life, death, and everything in between.

Until she opened her eyes properly and was on the road to recovery, I was questioning absolutely everything. I was definitely questioning my mental strength, and whether I had what it took to cope with whatever came next. But one thing I wasn't questioning was my faith.

I was brought up with religious teachings from my mum, and that opened my eyes to a lot of things. On the downside, the saddest thing about a lot of God's worshippers is that while you might meet an atheist who isn't judgemental of you and has a positive attitude to your life, you might easily meet a hardcore religious person who's the most judgemental person in the room. But the greatest thing about growing up in faith was that in the most troubling of times, and my darkest times, I felt that I had someone to talk to. And I didn't have to put my faith into a human – which is ideal when the only humans you can talk to might judge you, or not want to hear your worries. Humans can be hard work, but God never is. There are no secrets: He knows your thoughts, so you have no choice but to be totally straightforward with Him.

And He's been there for me. One time, I was in Stockwell Park Estate chilling and minding my own business when some guys came through the estate. One of them turned from the corner and both our sets of eyes made four: then they started shooting at me. I froze in front of a wall. He kept shooting my way. I closed my eyes and I said, simply: 'God?' That was it. The brick behind me was flickering, and brick dust was showering down onto me. It was so close, but I stayed frozen and just kept thinking of God. All the bullets were hitting the wall. There's no way that many bullets would normally have missed me. I truly believe it was God looking out for me that day.

Later on, after I'd moved to Essex, had almost been killed by the mould-infested flat, had ended up in hospital and had ended up back at my mum's house, I had a less frantic moment, but it was one where it also felt like my life was hanging in the balance. At that point I'd seen my music career almost take off, but I'd been smacked down again by the lung infection and was back in Brixton, back at square one, back to asking my mates if I could borrow money off them so I could eat. I sat in my mum's place in the kitchen and said, out loud: 'Fuck. I am so fucked. God fucking help me.' The good news is He didn't mind the bad language, because now look at me: a few years later I have two houses and there's no mould in either of them. He came through. Nobody can tell me my God's asleep.

Even in my older times, like now, if I have a funky situation where I feel weird, I can always go into my room, have a quiet moment and just pray. I'm so happy my mum and grandma instilled that in me. Human beings are always flawed, but God never is. Real talk.

Of course, it has to be a two-way relationship. Coming through for Him is a different thing altogether. A couple of nights ago I'd just got in from a gig – it was five o'clock in the morning and as I lay there I said quietly: 'God, thank you, for everything. Thank you for looking after my kids, for waking me up in the morning. For making me stable. Just, thank you.'

It wasn't a long, ten-page essay. It wasn't very loud either, because I didn't want to wake the missus. I just wanted to say thank you. He was there for me when my life was in danger and I was being shot at, and He was there for me when my life felt like it was on a shit spiral to oblivion. Now I'm comfortable with food in my fridge, money in my account and petrol in my car; my kids are fed, my dog's fucking fat, my missus is healthy. Everything seems alright now, and that's when it's even more important to say: 'Thank you'. That's the best kind of giving back: doing it when you don't even need to.

Having faith in God means I must also accept the presence of the Devil. The Devil takes many forms but he shows his true face when he needs to, and having been in the music industry for some time I'm sure I've met him more than once. The Devil is your desires and your weaknesses. He thrives most of all on people who think life has a shortcut. He's the shortcut master. Imagine there's a sign that says you'll have to walk fifty yards to get to your success, and then imagine the Devil appearing and telling you there's a side road that'll only be ten yards. He won't tell you the shortcut has loads of pit bulls in it. The reason for this is that the Devil is a cunt.

And he'll trick you into thinking you're on the path to Heaven, even when you're not. The most important thing is that if you decide to do something nice because you think that's what other people want, or because it looks better to the world that you're doing it, that's not gonna count as a blessing. You're still going to Hell. It doesn't make you a nice person if you're only doing something because you want to go to Heaven. You're trying to manipulate people. You're trying to manipulate God. A blessing comes from true and genuine and pure actions. So don't think that doing the occasional nice thing is going to save you from Hell. A serial killer could help an old lady across the road every couple of weeks, but doing a good thing doesn't make you a good person. When your judgement day comes, there's no hiding from the truth.

If someone told me there was some way I could look forward into the future to see the circumstances of my own death – proper cyclops shit, straight out of mythology – I think I'd want to know what was going to go down. But the reason I'd want to know is this: I'd want to show that I could prove them wrong. That's just my natural instinct: if someone shows you something negative, show them why they've got it wrong. But deep down I believe nobody other than God can tell you when it's your time to go. And when God wants to grab you, He'll grab you. My thing is this: I don't want to live forever. I just want to live appropriately, and for as long as God says I should live, and to do as much as I can in that time.

Some geezers have a full-on meltdown when they hit 30, but I don't mind the idea of getting older. I mean, I'm not saying getting older isn't pretty weird, particularly because I always thought I was going to die by the time I was 25 anyway, so at the ripe age of 34 I feel like I'm a grandad, and I'm officially now classed as an old G! Man's on the streets, living, when a lot of my mates haven't made it to this age. But as I get older, and look ahead to 40, 50 and what-ever comes after, I don't have any desire to resist my age.

You need to appreciate your age, and age gracefully. And obviously a lot of people in the public eye spend a lot of money changing their appearance so that they look younger, but they're not fooling other people and most of all they're not even fooling themselves. You can buy as many new faces as you want, but the truth is: you're old. Your insides can't lie. You can look 12 and have the organs of a 60-year-old – that's up to you. But I think you should embrace it all. When I'm 44 I want to look 44. And if I just so happen to still look 34 at that point then, well, what can I say? Black don't crack. My point is, playing God with yourself and trying to hold onto time: that's just not for me. I want to make the most of now, not hang on to then.

Imagine how tragic it would be if at 34 I was still trying to keep the lifestyle of a 22-year-old. We all know those people: the tragic ones in their forties trying to keep up with teenagers, pretending they're not old enough to be these kids' dads. You can't stay in just one era of your life forever. That's not life at all – that's fantasy. The essence of life is going through different eras and segments: kid; teenager;

first date; first kid; first grandkid. It's all life! If you held onto an early part, you'd never get to the next part. Life's supposed to be a journey.

The best thing to do in that time is appreciate life – and accept that you don't know everything. Some people get to a certain age and they think: 'I'm happy with how my life is now.' Everything just stops for them, but the rest of the world carries on. Other people, on the other hand, never stop being interested in life. People who realise they can learn stuff from younger people are the ones who are winning, and the fact is that when you hit 40 you probably know far less about the world than a 20-year-old. Kids absorb EVERYTHING.

Me? I never want to stop learning. I see my grandma as a great example of this. When my mum told me about growing up she would always talk about her own mum and how strict she was – and don't forget, my gran was a pastor, with her own church, so it was a very religious household with no naughty business tolerated. My mum was strict with me, but this was nothing on how strict her own mum had been with her. My mum always used to tell me: 'The stuff you get away with is unheard of!' But get this: I used to watch wrestling with my grandma. She used to whoop and clap, just like me, when Hulk Hogan was landing on some dude's head. I could have a totally laid-back relationship with her. Here's the thing: compared to some other people's nans who are very old school and traditional, my grandma evolved with the times. I remember when she told me she wanted a Facebook account! When you're willing to evolve, there's no way you'll go extinct.

Eventually, if I get to the age of 70, maybe I'll relax a little. I'm excited to get proper old, truth be told. When I look ahead to that age I see a simple scene: I'm not in the city at that point, I'm in the countryside with no nosy neighbours where it's nice and quiet, but with good transport links to where the action is. I never want to feel too isolated from what's going on in the world. And I'll spend my days wisely: I'll spend plenty of quality time with the grandkids at the weekend and I'll have tonnes of Viagra in my mansion, because during the week I'll be having sex with all my carers. I'll be living my best life. And when my grandchildren ask me how to live their lives, I'll say: 'Education is power, but so is common sense. Some kid who's been to Eton might have the qualifications, but he's thick as shit, and you need to get the right balance. Be your own leader and your own warrior.'

But the big D comes to all of us, and by that I mean death, not dick. The surest thing in the world is death, and I've experienced so much of it during my lifetime that I'm kind of numb to it. I'm not saying it doesn't hit me in the gut every time I encounter it, but the irony is after your third or fourth experience around death it just becomes part of life.

I've seen young people die, I've seen old people die; I've seen man drop dead at 40 when they don't drink, don't smoke, and go to the gym five times a week, while people who smoke like chimneys their entire lives live to a ripe old age. The fact that you can live how you're told to live then die anyway changes how you think. You could leave this earth early for any reason. Freak of nature, bizarre kitchen accident, anything. The important thing is to make your time here count. All that matters is that you've lived the best you can while you're on this earth.

And then? Well, the depiction of Heaven has preoccupied scholars and artists for centuries but from my point of view I'm expecting weed everywhere – like, weed *everywhere* – with some buff chicks.

None of us really understands what happens after death. There are things I believe because I'm a religious person, but even if you're not religious I ask you this: do you believe this is the only dimension we're in? Do you really believe there's no spiritual energy around us, beyond the world we're in? Wherever you're reading this, I want you to ask yourself: how would you feel if a ghost walked in now? What would you say to it? How would you react to what it said back? Would you fear it, or embrace its presence?

If you're picturing that scene, there's part of you that believes ghosts might exist.

And I can tell you this, I definitely believe they exist. I know that because I've seen one. A few years back I did a show at Tokyo World in Bristol and the organisers put me up for the night in this fancy hotel – a proper wine-drinking, over-18s place with these mad wavy rooms where the bedside tables cost more than all the furniture in your first flat put together. So man just don't feel easy in this place – my spiritual radar's telling me that this place just doesn't seem right. I phoned my boy Dullah who was in his room on another floor and said: 'Come on, bro, let's go downstairs for a smoke.'

And on the way down to meet him, just before the elevator, I saw this little white boy, no more than six or seven years old, with no T-shirt on and chequered pyjama trousers on his bottom half. He had blond hair in a fringe and he was screaming for his mum. 'MUM! MUM! MUM!' Now, it's two in the morning, I'm in the corridor with this kid, and my first thought is: 'There's a white boy out here screaming and crying with his shirt off, I'm a big black guy and I'm definitely not sticking around to explain my way out of this.' So I just walk past him – he doesn't even look at me – and get the lift down to reception.

I say to the guy on reception: 'Er, bruv, there's a boy upstairs screaming for his mum. This building's weird, blud. What's wrong with this place?'

'There's no way you saw a kid crying for his mum,' he says. 'There are no kids staying here – it's an adults-only hotel.'

My first thought: 'What the fuck?'

And then the guy goes, totally matter-of-fact: 'Oh, this hotel is on one of the local ghost trails. People come from all

over the country to stay here and on ghost-hunting weekends. So it's probably one of those.'

PROBABLY ONE OF THOSE!

Well, I totally shat it at that point! I got Dullah to
grab my stuff, chucked it in the car, left the hotel and
drove straight back to London. I'm happy to believe in
ghosts as a concept but I'm fucked if I'm staying in some
mad spooky hotel with one, no matter how good the room
service menu is.

Maybe I'll be more open to the day-to-day matters of
haunting if I ever become a ghost myself, but God willing
I've got a lot more life to live before I get to that stage.

And in life there are crunch times when you have to
choose what sort of person you're going to be. I've been
faced, more times than I care to remember, with the choice:
what type of man am I, and what type do I want to become?

And there have been a few options. There's your
'passer-by' man: that man who leaves about as much
impression on the world as a fart. He'll be born, he'll pass
by, then he'll die and nobody will care. At the other end
of the spectrum there are men who are righteous in terms
of morals, deeds and ways of action; those men are never
really liked in their lifetimes, because having morals and
decency shows other people what their own flaws are. Then
there's the scummy bummy man – the type that hates to be
shown up by the righteous man. I think deep down every
man wants to live their life with morals and pride, but some

people think you can take shortcuts to get there, as if you can pick these qualities off a shelf when it suits you, and that's where the scumminess and the bumminess comes in. You'll also find that there are Peter Pans: the men who never grow up, who are 65 in age and 12 in mentality, and who don't realise that being of age doesn't make you a man, or that being old is not the same thing as being wise. The last type is the fucking idiot.

I suppose you could say I've been all these men at one point or another, as life's thrown its endless barrage of shit my way. The pain of motherfucking life is something it's never easy to process. For me it was a confusing pain: being a poor kid not understanding why he was poor, and not understanding why life was how it was. That sort of pain stays with you. I'm doing so well right now, but there are days when it still feels like I'm suffering.

But then, everyone has their own pains. My mum finished school when she was eight years old; she had to look after all her brothers and sisters because my nan was ill, and she only learned to read and write after she'd had my brother. Yet she still managed to work and make a good life and teach me principles and ideas that I now use in my life today. And where I am today, I'm proud to say, is in a position where things are popping off for the right reasons, meaning that my mum can hold her head up high, and for the first time in decades she's no longer known by her first name down at Brixton police station. I've found that so much in life comes down to how you look after your family, your mates, and even people you're meeting for the first time and might never meet again. To look after them, you've got to look after yourself.

And if there is something you don't like about yourself, what the fuck are you going to do about it? Be a little baby about it, or get it sorted? I know it's easy when you're young not to see a future, and to have to explain to your parents: 'I'm following the dream.' But you have to be brave. You need the confidence to be able to go for it, whatever other people are saying. I always think of the morning when I was six when I woke up and decided I was going to learn how to do kick-ups. How many times did I put that ball on my foot and try to keep it in the air? It went down every time. I was in the garden for hours. Then I got it on smash and decided I was the black Eric Cantona. Whether you're a footballer or anyone else, one thing that's true in life is that you miss every shot you don't take.

And yeah, sometimes you're going to drop the ball. Sometimes you'll get tackled so hard that you'll be on your arse watching someone else hoof your ball over the back fence. But rejection is part of life, just as much a part as winning. When I see people playing God and choosing which parts of life they want I see people who don't under-stand that without rejection and disappointment, there's no way of knowing what happy really feels like, and no way of knowing what it's like to fight and thrive and get yourself to a better place. After six months of a perfect life, you'd almost give anything for a catastrophe!

If you've got something wrong and you know it's your fuck-up and why, then sure, you can figure out how to fix it. If it remains a mystery, you'll fuck up again and again. You'll always get in the same predicament. Learning from mistakes isn't a bad thing; making the same mistake twice is the problem. But what's life without ups and downs? How do you learn to appreciate something good if nothing bad has ever happened to you? If everything's great all the time, how can you have a better day than the day before? You'd never know how it is to think: 'I'm chuffed.'

The thing is, I came from a shithole. And I ain't going back. I refuse to go back. I refuse to be the story people tell each other: 'Do you remember when Narstie had that house, that watch, that car?' I own all my jewellery; it's safely in a box. I haven't had to pawn anything and God willing it will stay that way. People sometimes forget that the person you are when you're 14 isn't the same person you are when you're 24 … 34 … 44. We change. Sometimes the changes are so small and so gradual we don't even notice them happening. Sometimes we need to force ourselves to change overnight. But change is no bad thing. Actually, it's the best thing you can ever hope for.

Every time we look in the mirror we see different sides of ourselves. You can see your younger self, your teenage self and your older self. The person you've been; the person you want to be. It was rare, back in the day, that I'd see the person I was there and then, in that minute. Sometimes I didn't want to see him. But now, when I look in the mirror, I see me. When I look in the mirror, I'm reminded that there were certain situations I went through that I thought I'd never survive.

But I also think: 'Rah, you surprise me. You did get through it. You're stronger than you ever thought you were.'

Whoever you are, wherever you're reading this and whatever your future's looking like, I know you're stronger than you think you are, too.

I hope you've enjoyed this book and learned a thing or two about me, the world we each live in, and the world you're going to build for yourself.

(And if you've learned nothing, all I can say is please recycle responsibly.)